"So many books make the history and practice of Christian spirituality dreadfully boring through their earnestness, but Jana Riess brought a smile to my face on page one! *Flunking Sainthood* is a witty memoir of a year of failing—and therefore, paradoxically, succeeding—at putting Jesus first. Would that we all failed so well."

—Tony Jones, author of *The Sacred Way: Spiritual Practices for Everyday Life*

"Who would have guessed that trying and failing at the spiritual disciplines is way better than not trying at all? And—here's the real surprise: it may even be better than trying and feeling like a success. *Flunking Sainthood* guides you into the human side of the spiritual life with good humor and a bathtub full of grace."

—Brian McLaren, author of *Naked Spirituality: A Life with God in 12 Simple Words*

"Warm, light-hearted, and laugh-out-loud funny, Jana Riess may indeed have flunked sainthood, but this memoir assures us that she is utterly and deeply human, and that is something even more wonderful. Honest and sincere, she will endear you from page one."

—Donna Freitas, author of *The Possibilities of Sainthood*

"*Flunking Sainthood* allows those of us who have attempted new spiritual practices, and failed, to breathe a great sigh of relief and to laugh out loud. Jana Riess's exposé of her year-long and less-than-successful attempts at eleven classic spiritual practices entertains and educates us with its honesty and down-to-earthiness. She writes in the unfiltered, uncensored way I'd write if I had the skill and the guts."

—Sybil MacBeth, author of *Praying in Color*

"Jana Riess's new book is a delight—fun, funny, engaging and a powerful reminder that the greatest work in our lives is not what we'll do for God but what God is doing in us."

—Margaret Feinberg, author of *Scouting the Divine* and *Hungry for God*

"Jana Riess proves to be a standup historian well-practiced in the art of oddly revivifying self-deprecation. This book is freaking wonderful—a candid and committed tale that resists supersizing and spirituality that has no home save the glory and muck of the everyday."

—David Dark, author of *The Sacredness of Questioning Everything*

JANA RIESS

flunking sainthood

A Year of Breaking the Sabbath, Forgetting to Pray, and Still Loving My Neighbor

PARACLETE PRESS
BREWSTER, MASSACHUSETTS

Flunking Sainthood: A Year of Breaking the Sabbath, Forgetting to Pray, and Still Loving My Neighbor

2011 First printing

Copyright © 2011 by Jana Riess

ISBN 978-1-55725-660-7

Unless otherwise designated, Scripture references are taken from the New Revised Standard Version Bible, copyright © 1989 by the Division of Education of the National Council of Churches of Christ in the U.S.A., and are used by permission. All rights reserved.

Scripture quotations marked (KJV) are taken from the Authorized King James Version of the Holy Bible.

Scripture quotations marked (NIV) are taken from the Holy Bible, New International Version®, NIV®. Copyright © 1973, 1978, 1984, 2011 by Biblica, Inc.™ Used by permission. All rights reserved worldwide.

Library of Congress Cataloging-in-Publication Data

Riess, Jana.
  Flunking sainthood : a year of breaking the Sabbath, forgetting to pray, and still loving my neighbor / Jana Riess.
      p. cm.
  Includes bibliographical references (p.   ).
  ISBN 978-1-55725-660-7 (paper back)
  1. Spiritual life—Christianity. 2. Perfection—Religious aspects—Christianity. 3. Failure (Psychology)—Religious aspects—Christianity. 4. Success—Religious aspects—Christianity. 5. Riess, Jana. 6. Spiritual biography. I. Title.
  BV4501.3.R537 2011
  248.4—dc23   2011022595

10 9 8 7 6 5 4 3 2 1

Published by Paraclete Press
Brewster, Massachusetts
www.paracletepress.com

Printed in the United States of America

FOR PHIL

my resident saint

AND FOR PAPA

who is such a blessing to us

Many people genuinely do not want to be saints, and it is probable that some who achieve or aspire to sainthood have never felt much temptation to be human beings.

—GEORGE ORWELL

contents

My mom is the sort of person who always wants to know how a book ends before committing to it. It's one of the only things I dislike about her, but she's part of a whole cadre of like-minded readers who furtively skip to the end of a book to spill its secrets before they make an emotional investment.

So for Mom, and for her silent but guilty compatriots, here is the spoiler: I am going to fail at every single spiritual practice I undertake in this book.

I didn't set out to write a book about spiritual failure. This project originated as a lighthearted effort to read spiritual classics while attempting a year of faith-related disciplines like fasting, Sabbath keeping, chanting, and the Jesus Prayer. It culminated in a year-end meeting with my editor, Lil Copan, in which I tried to steel her for the fact that I had fallen short in every single spiritual practice I'd tried. I felt dejected—what kind of loser fails at the Jesus Prayer? I mean, it's twelve words long and takes about four seconds to recite. Lil helped me see the value in a different kind of book, one about the wild acceptability of failure itself. She suggested the title *Flunking Sainthood*. I'm grateful to her for careful editing, challenging feedback, and broad vision. (Even as I write that sentence, I hear her voice in my head, telling me I've used excessive adjectives.) I'm grateful also to Jon Sweeney, Carol Showalter, Pamela Jordan, Sister Mercy, Jenny Lynch, and all the good people at Paraclete Press, a bright spot on the landscape of publishing.

I owe thanks to Beliefnet.com for helping me find my tribe of failed saints through the "Flunking Sainthood" blog, and to the many folks I've talked to at Emergent gatherings who connected immediately with the idea of finding the joy in failure. Jonathan Merkh provided invaluable help with my book contract, and many people recommended books to me, including Cynthia Eller, Bob Fryling, and Jeanette Thomason. Jamie Noyd and Leighton Connor, members of my writing group, offered invaluable feedback on drafts, and the sisters at the Community of Jesus spoiled me with exceptional food and hospitality while I was on my writing retreat. My family deserves a medal for graciously loving me through another book.

This book arose out of conversations with many generous friends and acquaintances, some of whom you'll meet on these pages, but especially Dawn and Andrew Burnett, Claudia Mair Burney, Rudy Faust, Donna Freitas, Nancy Hopkins-Greene, Asma Hasan, Kelly Hughes, Ron and Debra Rienstra, Scot McKnight, Lauren Winner, and Vinita Hampton Wright.

My December practice of generosity would not have been possible without the financial contributions of Christopher Bigelow, Samuel Brown, Alethea Teh Busken, Stephen Carter, Lil Copan, David Dobson, Sheryl Fullerton, Kathryn Helmers, Myra Rubiera Hinote, Kelly Hughes, Donna Kehoe, Mark Kerr, Linda Hoffman Kimball, Tania Rands Lyon, Sheri Malman, Preston McConkie, Don McKim, Jana Muntsinger, Marcia Z. Nelson, Kerry Ulm Ose, Tina Hebbard Owen, Vince Patton, Charles Randall Paul, Bernadette Price, Jana Bouck Remy, John Nakamura Remy, Phyllis Riess, Carol Showalter, Kristen Mueller Smith, Megan Moore Smith, Rory Swenson, Hargis Thomas, and Debbie Wilson Waggoner.

I hope I haven't forgotten anyone, but this is a book about screwing up, so I give myself a pass.

choosing practices

You see that I am a very little soul
who can offer to God only very little things.
—ST. THÉRÈSE OF LISIEUX

My friend Kelly went through a phase when she was about seven years old when she wanted quite desperately to be a nun. In the flush of religiosity attending her First Communion, she pictured herself in a sweeping black habit like the sisters who taught at her strict elementary school. Actually, I just made that last part up. Kelly was a kid after Vatican II, so the nuns probably wore jeans with holes at the knees and chain-smoked in the teachers' lounge. I'll have to ask her sometime. But the *Sound of Music* image makes for a better story.

I didn't grow up Catholic, or any other religion for that matter. My dad was an angry atheist who considered religion a crutch for people who were too stupid to know any better. My mom was considerably more charitable but no more interested in organized religion than she was in volunteering for a Stalinist gulag. So it's hard to explain why I was always drawn inexorably toward religion and religious people.

As a child, I looked forward to spending a Saturday night at my friend Gretchen's house not only for the thrill of staying up past midnight but also because, no matter what time we nodded off, we had to wake up early on Sunday to attend services at her downtown

Lutheran church. I loved dressing up in different clothes on Sunday, sneaking multiple donuts during the coffee klatch, and learning Bible stories on flannel board. This innate religiosity followed me through childhood. Even when I was away from home for two weeks each summer at Girl Scout camp, I'd attend both the Saturday evening Catholic Mass and the Sunday morning Protestant worship. At home, I talked several times to the friendly, guitar-playing Reform Jewish rabbi at my friend Sara's synagogue. At ten, it seemed a good idea to keep all my options open.

But for twenty-five years now I've been a Christian, having sealed the deal with Jesus at a snowy winter youth group retreat during my freshman year of high school. In tears, freezing my ass off on a rock, I stared up at the stars and talked out loud to God like a crazy person. A peace washed over me when I knew God had marked me as *his* crazy person. That was it. I was no longer an outsider looking in on God's family; I had a place at the table. I just didn't know then that it would be impossible to maintain the same passion for God I felt at that singular moment.

I feel little romance for religion anymore. I don't yearn for quiet time alone with Jesus or think about him every hour. These days, Jesus and I are like old marrieds—sometimes I'm a nag, and sometimes he is emotionally distant. Maybe the extremes I'm contemplating with a year of bizarre faith practices are the spiritual equivalent of greeting Jesus at the door wrapped only in cellophane. I'm trying to pop a little zing back into our relationship.

I should backtrack and explain. I am about to embark on an adventure. At the suggestion of some publisher friends, I am conducting a year-long experiment into reading the spiritual classics. Although reading was the extent of their original idea, I immediately upped the ante to include a corresponding monthly spiritual practice to supplement the reading. I guess I am an overachiever.

But which practices? And which spiritual classics? Everyone, it seems, has an opinion. My girlfriend Donna tells me that she absolutely will not be my friend anymore if I don't spend at least one month reading Augustine. Since she's Catholic, she pronounces this August-*eeen*, and since she's the brainy by-product of about a kajillion years of Catholic education, she has strong opinions about his books. "Read *The Confessions!*" she exclaims. "No, read *City of God!* That's a really good one, and it's so neglected."

I'm not that interested in *City of God*, preferring more personal tales I can relate to. I decide to start with Thérèse of Lisieux, having bypassed Augustine in the hopes that Donna was speaking in the passion of the moment and will still be my friend even if I ignore the guy from Hippo. I spend much of January reading Thérèse's memoir, *The Story of a Soul*. The nineteenth-century French saint Thérèse is famous for bringing saintly wisdom down to the level of the hoi polloi, for calling herself the least of the saints—just an uncultivated "Little Flower" among all of God's gorgeous roses. I figure I can relate.

It doesn't go quite as planned, however. Instead of being the perfect kickoff to my year of trying to be a saint, the book makes me want to strangle the Little Flower. I'm puzzled by why so many people love Thérèse. In her memoir she calls herself "very expansive," which is one of the great understatements of hagiography. In our day we might use different words: *drama queen*. Thérèse decided at an early age that she was going to be a nun, and nothing would deter her. She was so bound for holiness that she went over her

Don't call me a saint.
I don't want to be dismissed that easily.
—DOROTHY DAY

priest's head to the bishop to get permission to enter the convent in her early teens. When both the priest and the bishop failed to comply with her wishes, she actually went all the way up the chain of command to the pope himself and charmed his socks off in a personal audience. Actually, do popes wear socks? I do not know.

At any rate, the pope waived the age requirement for Thérèse so she could get her way and be the first in her class to join a convent. In the end, it might have been a good thing too, because Thérèse died in her early twenties of some appropriately nineteenth-century disease like consumption. But at least she had fulfilled her convent fantasy before she started wasting away in her cell. The book she left behind has inspired millions with its central idea that ordinary people can become "saints" too, wherever they are. I'm determined that this idea, at least, is something positive I will take away from Thérèse, even though I find her manipulative behavior annoying and have made a poor job of reading her book.

It's helpful that Thérèse left behind some instructions about DIY sainthood for ordinary people, because in my own quest for sainthood, I'm not planning to join a convent, wheedle the pope, or contract tuberculosis. In fact, I start keeping a list of extremes to which I will not go:

✓ I will not climb to the top of a pole and live there. Simeon the Stylite did this for thirty-seven years, actually strapping himself to the pole so he wouldn't topple over when he fell asleep. I have zero interest in doing this. My bed is just fine.

✓ I will not allow myself to be devoured by lions, like the early Christian martyr Felicitas. To be on the safe side, I will avoid all large arenas for the year. Also zoos.

✓ I refuse to pluck out my own eyes for God. Legend has it that St. Lucia did this, then put her eyes on a plate and gave them to the fiancé she had Dear Johned in order to pursue a life with God. *So* not happening here.

✓ I will not strip naked and parade in the town square. St. Francis did this, but that was in Europe, where they also have nude beaches.

But if the opportunity arises, I will remain open to the following:

✓ Magically bilocating. St. Drogo was allegedly able to achieve this, appearing in two places at once. This was not such a boon for others, however, as the afflicted Drogo is considered the Patron Saint of Unattractive People. Still, bilocation would be an enviable superpower in the harried twenty-first century. Sign me up.

✓ Hanging out my shingle as a miracle worker, free of charge. Who wouldn't want a miracle nowadays?

Although miracle working sounds exciting, I think that my spiritual practices will be more tried-and-true—like, say, prayer. I'm lousy at it and could use a whole new prayer MO. In lieu of fancy powers like bilocation, I'd be thrilled just to feel like God was accepting my calls.

I also plan a month to focus on reading the Bible, which is hardly going to win an extreme spirituality competition. But these tamer practices fit well with family considerations. I don't want my year of radical spirituality to be a hardship on my loved ones, though some amount of sacrifice on their part is inevitable. At least, this is what I try to tell my husband, Phil, when we are lying in bed one night in January and I outline the year for him.

"What I'm thinking," I announce, "is that there will be a month where I fast, and a month where I try not to spend money, and a month where I observe an Orthodox Sabbath." I can tell that he is listening, but in a halfhearted way as he attends to his Sudoku puzzle. I drop the bombshell.

"And then, of course, there has to be a month where I don't have any sex," I explain matter-of-factly. "That will be in November."

"Okay. Uh huh." There is a pause before his head snaps over to me with an alarmed expression. "No, wait, what did you say?"

"I said that in order for this to be authentic, there has to be a month where I give up sex. I mean, look at all the saints. Most of them were celibate their whole adult lives. Abstaining for a month is the least I can do. I think I can make it, so long as I have chocolate."

I'd rather laugh with the sinners than cry with the saints; the sinners are much more fun.
—BILLY JOEL

"But . . . but . . . " I definitely have his full attention now. "Are you serious?"

It would be great fun to see how long I can keep this going, but eventually I put him out of his misery and admit that I'm bluffing. He is immensely relieved, which makes me realize I've scored one point at least: anything else I subject the poor man to this year will seem like small potatoes compared to the forced celibacy I could have inflicted upon him. I will remind him of this fact should his enthusiasm for my project ever flag.

Even though I don't quite know where this project is taking me or what this year will bring, I'm glad that I've decided to bring spirituality down to earth by trying to actually live it and not just read about it. In her book *Mudhouse Sabbath*, Lauren Winner points out a scene in Exodus 24 where the Israelites get the Ten Commandments and promise to obey God. The odd part of the story is the word order of their response: "All that you have said we will do and hear." *Wait a minute*, we think. *Shouldn't that be the other way around? How can we do what God commands until we've heard it first?* Some biblical scholars say this is just a scribal error, and it's certainly possible that we're all reading too much into this particular bout of biblical dyslexia. But I prefer the rabbinic explanation Lauren gives: some rabbis have taught that we can't really *hear* what God is saying, or let it sink into our souls and beings, until we have tried to *do* what God is saying. The practice precedes the belief, not the other way around. Interesting. It's like what Abraham Joshua Heschel, a rabbi we'll meet again in chapter 7, has to say about spiritual practice. Although he's speaking here specifically of Jewishness, it's applicable to spiritual practice for everyone:

> A Jew is asked to take a *leap of action* rather than a *leap of thought*. He is asked to surpass his needs, to do more than he understands in order to understand more than he does. In carrying out the word of the Torah he is ushered into the presence of spiritual meaning. Through the ecstasy of deeds he learns to be certain of the hereness of God.

I'm not sure I'll be feeling much of the "ecstasy of deeds," but I do know there's a common thread in the Hebrew Bible/Old Testament of walking with God. Enoch and Noah (Gen. 5 and 6) were righteous because they *walked with God*, not because they believed the right things about God or passed an orthodoxy litmus test. (Just FYI, in the interest of full biblical disclosure: the Bible makes this observation about Noah's righteousness *before* the guy gets totally wasted and curses one of his sons. After Vineyardgate, the Bible has no comment about Noah.) Walking with God comes up again in Deuteronomy 10, in the Exodus, and in Micah 6:8, one of my favorite Scriptures. To paraphrase, Micah says God has already shown us what is good: to do justice, to love kindness, and to walk humbly with God. I like that. This year is going to be

fasting in the desert

A fat stomach never breeds fine thoughts.
— ST. JEROME

5:57 PM. I'm seated in a straight-back wooden chair at a suburban Cracker Barrel, counting the minutes until the sun sets at 6:04 and I can break my fast. Say what you want about the Cracker Barrel, but when the chips are down, it's the soul food of any self-respecting Midwesterner. You can keep your arugula and sashimi. Pass me the mashed potatoes.

"Could you please bring the biscuits before the meal? And some jam? And a glass of chocolate milk?" I congratulate myself on keeping the edge of desperation out of my voice.

"Sure thing, hon. Be right back," promises the waitress as she dashes away. However, she doesn't return for a full fifteen minutes. The place is jammed with customers, and the smell of their meatloaf overpowers my senses as I gesture unsuccessfully to recapture her attention. I busy myself with my iPhone and try not to notice each minute ticking past on the digital clock in its top right corner. ,

"I'm *so* sorry, hon. We got slammed all of a sudden," the waitress apologizes as she shoves various items on the table. I smile her way but don't speak because I've already crammed a biscuit in my mouth.

I demolish the bread, the milk, and what passes for vegetables at the Cracker Barrel. Nothing has ever tasted so delicious.

I hate fasting. How am I going to make it through a month of this?

This month, for my first grand experiment, the plan is to read the Desert Fathers and Mothers about fasting and see what wisdom the ancient sages might have to offer me, a relative newbie to this ancient art. The Desert Parents were some of the first hermits of the Christian tradition. We call them "parents," but that's only in a spiritual sense; they were celibate monks and nuns of the third century onward who fled family life and the city so they could meet God out in the hinterlands. They lived simply, selling all their possessions, and they usually embraced solitude. Or at least, they tried to. Solitude was hard to come by, because some of the Desert Parents were like rock stars in their day. Ordinary folks had the annoying habit of knocking on their caves for marital advice, miraculous healings, or a nice pithy aphorism or two. And such intrusions were actually a good thing, because sometimes the groupies took the trouble to write down the Desert Parents' teachings.

As ascetics, the Desert Mothers and Fathers had a great deal to say about fasting, and I'll be reading those teachings this month. But the twist is that I am going to do the Christian fast like a Muslim during Ramadan. Although I like the Desert Parents in theory, I'm not keen to emulate their actual fasting practices, which included severe self-denial. Some didn't eat or drink for days or even weeks on end. This seems to me like an engraved invitation for psychosis, so I'll pass. I need a more moderate fasting practice that I can implement from day to day. I've always admired the annual Muslim tradition of fasting from sunup to sundown and wondered if I could do it. This is my chance to put it into practice. It seems far more sensible than outright starvation.

It's no accident that fasting is going to be the first spiritual practice I attempt. I'd love to tell you that I plotted out my year in this way because I was so excited to fast that I simply couldn't wait. But the real reason I wanted to do this discipline early in the year is because if you're fasting from sunup to sundown, what better time to do this than in winter when the days are short? And at just twenty-eight days, February is the briefest month on the calendar.

I need to become vigilant about the times the sun rises and sets, so I begin my pre-February preparation by checking online for a sun calendar for Cincinnati. On the first day of the month, I plan to get up around six o'clock to have time for a huge breakfast before sunup. The days will get a little longer as the month wears on, which means I'll have to get up earlier each morning and break the fast later each evening. But it's all right; I feel ready. I can do this. *Bring it on.*

While you are young and healthy, fast, for old age
with its weakness will come. As long as you can,
lay up treasure, so that when you cannot, you will be at peace.
— S Y N C L E C T I C A

BOOT CAMP

It turns out that "bring it on" is not the most humble, spiritual phrase with which to begin a fast. Although I commence with the enthusiasm of a zealot, by the middle of the second day I'm hungry enough to call it quits and devour everything in the refrigerator.

In my church we fast once a month, but it's always on a Sunday, which means I'm not expected to produce coherent thoughts or speeches, and I can usually accelerate the experience by taking a two-hour nap in the afternoon. Fasting on a weekday is a whole different kettle of fish. I feel fuzzy and unfocused as I answer e-mails and craft a report. The positive side of not taking an hour off for lunch is that I have more time to work, and am in fact itching for something like work to stop my brain from thinking about food. The downside is that it's difficult to concentrate. I'm starting to curse one of the things I've always loved about our neighborhood—the proximity of great restaurants right around the corner. I can smell naan baking, and what I guess to be curry.

Time passes slowly, the clock as slothful as my own body. "I don't know if I can do this," I complain on day three to a Muslim friend who fasts like this every year. "I'm so hungry and tired all the time." I sound whiny even to my own ears, and feel about six years old. And I can't even think about the faith-related reasons I'm supposed to be fasting; I don't feel any closer to God and haven't experienced any of the Desert Parents' promised fonts of spiritual wisdom. I'm just trying to get through each day without cheating on the fast or strangling someone. It seems a tall order.

"It will get better," she promises. "It's normal to feel exhausted at first. A lot of people take naps during the day if they can."

No kidding. I feel like I've been given narcotics. I'm grateful to work from home, and start shifting my work schedule to accommodate an afternoon nap during my former lunch hour.

One area where fasting cramps my style is in my writing. I love to write at cafés, with a mug of hot chocolate, noise-canceling headphones, and two hours without the interruptions of editing or family life. But what's the coffeehouse protocol for moochers? Could I go to the café, order something, and then stare at it like a wounded puppy for two hours? Or should I tell Tony, the friendly proprietor of the Coffee Emporium, that I am riding on the coattails of his Wi-Fi this month but have no intention to purchase anything for four weeks? Neither option sounds appealing, so I reconfigure my work life to write from home with only partial success. I feel vaguely housebound.

On day five, I hit my Waterloo. I have to commute into the office for meetings. Because I wake up late, I eat breakfast quickly, cramming shredded wheat cereal with blueberries into my mouth in a mad race against the colors in the sky. But by the end of my two-hour drive, I'm already hungry, and I have more than nine hours to go until sunset. It's an awful day—the weather is appalling, I can't silence my growling stomach, and I feel cold from head to toe. I wear my wool coat almost all day as I sit in meetings, musing on the truth of at least one thing I've read: fasting lowers a human being's core body temperature. Hypothesis confirmed. I am now a science experiment.

Why did anyone ever imagine that there was anything spiritual about fasting? This is boot camp. It feels punitive and harsh.

The very next morning, though, brings a breakthrough. Before dawn, I meet my friend Jamie for a blowout breakfast at IHOP, indulging in an omelet with toast and hash browns. Even though I can't finish the enormous omelet, I find that it's enough to see me through the day. Miracles and wonders! Six PM comes and I don't feel crabby or exhausted.

In fact, I am a bit elated. The South Beach Dieters must be on to something: protein does make a difference in staving off hunger.

I'm not sure if it's the new approach to breakfast or just the fact that my body has adjusted to the feast-or-famine food schedule, but things begin to look up. I have energy again. In fact, I have more energy than I'm used to in the dead of winter, the season when darkness creeps forward to gate-crash my life. The worst part is always the lack of sunlight, of rising in shadows and pushing through the long winter evenings. This year, by contrast, I welcome the redemptive darkness as a friend. Darkness is when the comforts of life—sleep and food—are most available to me. As I settle into a rhythm of the fast, I feel like I've conquered the DTs enough after the first week that I'm ready to think about spiritual questions. So far, my fast has been more like an episode of *Survivor* than a religious quest, with little energy for anything but getting through the day. It's time to go deeper.

FASTING WITH THE DESERT PARENTS

"So, have you had any visions yet?" a Christian friend asks me in my second week of fasting.

"Only of casseroles," I reply, trying to keep things lighthearted. In truth I am surprised by the question, and by the fact that it keeps coming up. Several people want to know whether it's true that fasting engenders trippy visions of God or the devil.

It's not true, at least for me, but there's a part of me that wishes for some dramatic manifestation, a divine response to this sacrifice. There's certainly a tradition in Christianity that shows God visiting people with extraordinary spiritual visions when they fast. Whether that's from calorie-deprived hallucination or a heightened spiritual sensitivity is anyone's guess.

But if there's too much emphasis on the fantastic, some of the fault lies with the Desert Parents, a number of whom were extremists. In history, the timing of the Desert Parents' exodus into the hinterlands of Egypt in the third and fourth centuries happened not long after the Roman Empire stopped killing Christians for sport. Were some of these Fathers and Mothers the same types who would have gladly served God by becoming lunch for lions? Maybe when the extremists were deprived of these more sudden and public routes to martyrdom, they skipped town for the desert and a new life of hermithood. One of them allegedly subsisted on the nutrients of a single pea, praising God for the miracle. They strove to model themselves after John the Baptist. I hate to remind them that things didn't exactly end well for John.

Other Desert Parents, thankfully, took a more middle-of-the-road approach, so these are the ones I focus on. Gregory the Theologian wrote, "There are three things that God requires of all the baptized: right faith in the heart, truth on the tongue, and temperance in the body." I chew on that list several times before committing it to my quote book. It sounds so sane. Doable, even. Cultivate faith; tell the truth; don't be ruled by your appetites. There's still plenty of room in that configuration for enjoying life to the fullest and loving family and friends. These are words to live by.

I also like the attitude of Theodora of the Desert. Theodora was a renowned ascetic in the late third century; monks and other people would travel from afar to hear her wisdom. Once the wife of a high-ranking tribune, she renounced all her wealth and position and died a penniless beggar. If anyone could have exercised a little puffery about fasting, it would be Theodora; she was an expert. But she didn't teach that. Instead, she told a story about a desert monk who had learned the secret to banishing demons. Would fasting make them go away, he asked the demons? No dice. "We do not eat or drink," replied the demons. Was it all-night prayer vigils, then? Nope—the demons did not require sleep. How about separation from the world? Hardly. If the demons were having this conversation with the monk out in the desert, hadn't they already followed him to the back of beyond? Then the demons released their bombshell: "Nothing can overcome us, but only humility." Mother Theodora wanted her listeners to know that while fasting, prayer, and abstinence from the world were all very well, those practices could easily be perverted into self-righteousness and dead legalism if done for the wrong reasons.

The Desert Parents suggest that humility is the key to godly fasting. When a student asked the Desert Father Moses (not the Bible's Moses—this was centuries later) what use fasting might be, Moses

Start by doing what is necessary, then do what's possible;
and suddenly you are doing the impossible.
—ST. FRANCIS OF ASSISI

replied, "It makes the soul humble." That's it. Fasting is not for visions or even for answers to prayer. It's not to manipulate God into acting according to our wishes, and not to show God just how willing we are to sacrifice something for him. Fasting is to help us on that painful road toward humility. That's why, in the Bible, so many of the instances of fasting occur hand in hand with mourning—the whole sackcloth-and-ashes bit.

MARS, VENUS, AND FASTING

As much as I like what the Desert Parents have to say about humility, fasting doesn't make me more humble and less worldly. In fact, all this single-minded focus on the body may be having the opposite effect.

"Have you lost much weight yet?" women ask me. Many of the women I talk to—even ones I consider to be profoundly spiritual—tell me right away, in tones that are simultaneously apologetic and defensive, that they "could never do that." Women admire the fasting but do not aspire to it. In contrast, many of the men seem to regard fasting as an extreme sport. They want to quantify my experience—How many days? How many pounds lost? Am I really abstaining from water as well as food? Several indicate they might want to try something similar. To them it's a competitive dare, like swallowing termites or jumping off a cliff. Something for the bucket list.

When it comes to fasting, men and women may be Mars and Venus. During my month of fasting, Brookhaven National Laboratory released an interesting study about gender and food deprivation. Scientists interviewed groups of men and women about their favorite foods before having them fast from all food overnight. The next day, the famished study participants were shown a parade of the foods they had identified as their favorites, all while hooked up to brain monitors. Both the men and the women reported that they were able to successfully utilize certain mind-over-matter "cognitive inhibition" techniques to suppress their hunger while they saw and smelled pizza, chocolate chip cookies, and other delights. However, it seems that the women lied. Whereas the men's brain scan results were consistent with what they reported—their brains were not responding in a dramatic way to the various food stimuli—the women reported being calm and collected while the food regions of their brains were actually hopping with exhilaration. "Even though the women said they were less hungry when trying to inhibit their response to the food, their brains were still firing away in the regions that control the drive to eat," said the lead scientist.

The reasons for this gender discrepancy are still unclear. Women's drive to eat may be related to the hormone estrogen, to socialized patterns of emotion, or to a more primal evolutionary drive to consume every last Oreo while it is around, since women have always been the primary feeders of the young. Whatever the reason, it seems to make obesity more of a potential issue for women, and fasting more of a hurdle.

You'd never know that, though, from reading some of the heroics of the crazy medieval women saints, several centuries after the Desert Parents. These women's fanaticism makes the Desert Mothers look positively domesticated. The most extreme saintly asceticism came in the Middle Ages, when the emaciated look was equated with greater holiness, especially for women. (It seems not much has changed in our culture's equating thinness with discipline and righteousness.) Medieval literature speaks glowingly of how these female saints languished for Jesus while their bodies wasted away to nothing. Although women account for only 17.5 percent of all saints who were canonized or venerated between the years 1000 and 1700, they account for 29 percent of saints known for "extreme austerities" like outrageous fasts and sleep deprivation.

Women also dominate the category of food-related miracles; some of these bony devotees spontaneously lactated and nursed without ever giving birth, while others reportedly emulated Jesus' miracle of feeding the five thousand with just a few loaves and fish. What does this mean for us? It means that fasting for all Christians can sometimes go too far, and that women in particular might need to be careful. It's a slippery slope. First you're trying out a simple fast, and the next thing you know you're like Hedwig of Silesia, levitating at the mere sight of the Eucharist, your gaunt body rising with ecstasy at the thought of a single morsel.

I reflect on all this fanaticism as I fast here in the twenty-first century, when tabloids are filled with news about which celebrity has shed her pregnancy pounds, and women's magazines, in bizarrely bipolar fashion, sport luscious layer cakes on the cover while promising surefire diet techniques in the pages within. It's a sad commentary on our weight-obsessed culture that we don't see the value of a fast for much except health and beauty. I critique the sentiment, chastising vanity and channeling my inner feminist to scourge the sexism of the diet culture, even while harboring a secret hope that maybe, in fact, I will drop a few pounds. Then I feel rotten about how worldly and vain I am, and determine not to diet, not to cast off a single ounce.

And yet it happens, even as I am eating Girl Scout cookies almost every night after dinner. I can hardly understand it, yet it is real, a bona fide postmodern miracle. The anti-manna. I am losing weight even while eating whatever the hell I want to for thirteen out of every twenty-four hours. Fasting is fabulous. I need to write a best-selling diet book.

"Wanna see something freaky?" I ask my husband and daughter, who are perched at the kitchen counter eating the supper I've prepared for them as I wait for the sun to go down. It's three weeks into the February fast. They confess that yes, they would love to see something freaky. And so I pull my pants down, right there in the kitchen, without even bothering to unbutton them. They slide right off. Jerusha is delighted by the transgressiveness of this unexpected act, and starts to laugh. Phil is startled and a little bit worried as he laughs along with her.

"Are you sure you're eating enough?" he asks.

"Yes, I think so," I reassure him. "It's not as dramatic as it seems. These are already my biggest jeans." But in my mind I am already thinking about The Box in the basement, the one that holds my B.J. jeans (Before Jerusha). I wonder if I could ever fit into those again?

I am simultaneously proud and ashamed of myself. In her excellent book on fasting, Lynne Baab talks about the hidden dangers of fasting in a diet culture, when we are fasting for some other reason than simply to grow closer to God. Some people, she argues, should never fast from food, and it's not just the usual suspects—pregnant or nursing moms, diabetics, the elderly, the infirm. She also exempts anyone who has ever struggled with an eating disorder, and admonishes yo-yo dieters who might be tempted to try crazy fasts for anything but spiritual purposes. I am particularly struck by what she says about the motives for fasting, which come down to a simple saying of Jesus: no one can serve two masters. If we're fasting for the secret purpose of weight loss, we aren't doing it with the singleness of heart that the Bible encourages.

As much as I get it, it's another thing to live it: I remain secretly pleased by the less matronly figure I spy in the mirror.

SO I'M FASTING ... WHY, EXACTLY?

If I'm not fasting for weight loss or self-improvement, why am I doing this? Some clarity comes when I read Scot McKnight's book *Fasting*, which challenges me to avoid fasting only in order to squeeze something spectacular out of God. McKnight wants Christians to move away from a spiritually immature idea of fasting (that is, to manipulate God into answering our prayers) to a more mature notion of focusing attention on God and letting worldly things fall away. McKnight objects to the whole "if A, then B" paradigm of fasting, calling Christians not to practice "instrumental fasting"—fasting with the idea of God as Santa Claus who will reward us if we're really, *really* good and don't eat all the cookies.

Fasting is not the means by which we are somehow turned into Aladdin and God is turned into our compliant genie, sent to grant our every wish. We must not think that by not eating we can have God eating out of our hand.
—LYNNE BAAB

I cheer for McKnight's argument but can't rise to that level of maturity. Maybe it's just too many years spent in a conservative church that at least implicitly teaches that when we fast, we can count on loads of good stuff coming our way: physical healings, answers to spiritual questions, divine guidance on relationships, the works.

What's more, I've experienced enough of those happy results myself that I can't just blithely dismiss them as a false use of fasting. Once, in my congregation, all of us fasted and prayed for a little boy who had been in a serious car accident. He recovered completely. What can I say? Yes, he was getting the best medical care; yes, he had a tremendously supportive family; and yes, maybe he would have pulled through no matter what. It's very possible that his recovery had nothing to do with the fact that two hundred people gave up food and drink so they could more completely concentrate their prayers for his recovery. But somehow, that explanation does not resonate with the wholly unscientific *feeling* I got about the affair. I felt a spiritual confirmation of how much God loved that kid, and that sense was somehow wrapped up in the greater closeness we all felt to God because of the fast.

So although I cringe when I hear simplistic theology that suggests that God will "honor" a fast by waving his fairy wand and granting whatever we ask just because we managed to spend a whole day without opening the refrigerator door, I admit there's also a part of me that wants my fasting to be precisely that effective and tangible. I wish that fasting *were* a viable means of supersizing my prayers, of making them jump the queue somehow so that they'd be shouted directly into God's right ear. It's ridiculous, and it's selfish, but I acknowledge the superstition and the selfishness even as that secret part of me wants to regard fasting as an efficacious form of magic. And so throughout the month I am praying: praying for a family member who's having a rough time, praying for the wife of a colleague who's been in a devastating car accident. Every time I feel a hunger pang—which is every few minutes most days—I send up a prayer.

A brother said to an old man: "There are two brothers. One of them stays in his cell quietly, fasting for six days at a time, and imposing on himself a good deal of discipline, and the other serves the sick. Which one of them is more acceptable to God?" The old man replied: "Even if the brother who fasts six days were to hang himself up by the nose, he could not equal the one who serves the sick."
—SAYINGS OF THE DESERT FATHERS

MISERY LOVES COMPANY

As I fast, I've been open about what I'm doing, whether it's explaining to colleagues why I'm eyeing their sandwiches greedily during a "working lunch" or announcing what I'll eat when I get to break my fast. After a couple of weeks of this, as I continue my research into what the Bible and church tradition have to say about fasting, I come across this New Testament passage that I've conveniently forgotten:

> And whenever you fast, do not look dismal, like the hypocrites, for they disfigure their faces so as to show others that they are fasting. Truly I tell you, they have received their reward. But when you fast, put oil on your head and wash your face, so that your fasting may be seen not by others but by your Father who is in secret; and your Father who sees in secret will reward you. (Matt. 6:16–18)

Well, damn. I'm barely halfway into this experiment and already I'm doing it wrong. Apparently the fast is supposed to be sub-rosa, a little secret between me and Jesus. I guess maybe this means I shouldn't have posted as my Facebook status things like, "I am about to break the fast!" or, "I have three long minutes until sunset." I might as well set up a soapbox in Pharisee Square and shout to the world how I thank God for being so righteous.

The thing is, though, that I can honestly say I never intended to call attention to my fast to earn frequent righteousness miles. It's more out of loneliness, actually. This whole month the most spiritually helpful day of fasting was actually the very first, and that was because it was an ordinary Fast Sunday at my church, when everyone else was fasting too. On the first Sunday of the month in my denomination, everybody fasts who is physically able to do so, and we donate the money we would have spent on food to help the poor. On that Sunday, I felt a solidarity with my fellow Christians that I haven't felt on any other day this month. Overall, it's been a very isolated journey.

It is not good for people to fast alone. I'm craving community almost as much as food. In the Orthodox Christian tradition, where literally half the year is made up of various sorts of fasts, the community factor is a given. "One can be damned alone, but saved only with others," goes a Russian Orthodox saying. Apparently it takes a village to raise a Christian.

As I near the end of February, I think about the dichotomy of what I clandestinely wanted from fasting—community—and what I chose to read this month: the Desert Parents, who are famous for *renouncing* community. Duh. The Desert Parents looked at fasting as the linchpin in a series of austere spiritual practices, which included sleeping on the ground (mentioned specifically by the Desert Mother Synclectica as beneficial) and celibacy. I don't intend to try either, nor am I interested in turning my back on the world. I *like* living in the world. I enjoy food and sex. And unlike the Desert folks, I'd be unhappy in a solitary life. I want my fasting to be a great big food-free party with everyone I know, where we all go hungry together. It occurs to me that the choice of Ramadan as a practice to emulate—a choice that seemed arbitrary at first—likely stems from a hidden jealousy I feel for the community that's created when a billion people around the world fast as one.

Although this month's spiritual classic wasn't always easy to relate to, it took reading the Desert Parents to realize that I don't wish to *be* them. That's good to know.

On my last night, I have to wait for twelve minutes after Phil and Jerusha have started eating before I'm allowed to pick up my knife and fork. This is it. I have made it. The fast is over.

Phil looks at me indulgently. "Don't ever, ever do this again," he pleads.

But I am not so sure. True, not one of the "things" I have been praying for has happened—my friend's wife remains in a coma, my family member is still struggling—and Jesus as Fairy Godmother has not officially recognized any sacrifice on my part. I'm no further on the journey to spiritual enlightenment or humility than I was twenty-eight days ago, which is discouraging. Yet physically, the fasting is so much easier than it was then. My body has adjusted to the new sleep schedule and to the absence of food during the day. There are still constant hunger pangs, but the feelings of weakness and bone-numbing cold that plagued me in the beginning have disappeared. Instead there are occasional glimmers of quiet elation and tranquility. I am more astonished by this than anyone.

"We'll see," I tell Phil. "Can you pass the chicken?"

meeting Jesus in the kitchen . . . or not

We can do little things for God; I turn the cake that is frying on the pan for love of him, and that done, if there is nothing else to call me, I prostrate myself in worship before him, who has given me grace to work; afterwards I rise happier than a king.

—BROTHER LAWRENCE

At first, I don't much like Brother Lawrence, the seventeenth-century French monk that everyone keeps telling me I need to read this month, as I attempt to infuse daily tasks with a sense of God's presence. Brother Lawrence is famous as a kind of cooking saint: assigned to kitchen duty for fifteen years in a monastery, he allowed his deep love for God to suffuse every meal he created, every pot he scrubbed.

I *try* to like him. It's just that he's so sanctimonious.

Part of my initial disconnect is the cultural divide that separates us. The book compiled from Brother Lawrence's letters and conversations, *The Practice of the Presence of God*, is one of those spiritual classics that thousands of people have read and been transformed by. But its language and tone are off-putting: I hate it that Brother Lawrence sometimes refers to himself in the third person. That may have been a post-Renaissance man's best shot at appearing humble, but nowadays it comes across as anything but. I'm also bothered by the relentless cheer of Brother Lawrence's opening pages. I mean, being European in the 1600s was not exactly a cocktail party: there were religious wars, beheadings, and smallpox outbreaks, all compounded by unfriendly realities like an absence of central heating and cable TV. Add to that some of the particular unpleasantness of monastic life: the 3 AM self-flagellations, the throwback medieval spoils system, the often-unreasonable abbots who were wealthy second sons with no special call to the brotherhood. I've watched every episode of *Cadfael*. I know how it was. But you'd never intuit any of that if you only had Brother Lawrence to rely upon, because the man was infuriatingly jolly. When he joined the monastery he'd been given numerous responsibilities, including all the icky chores that more established monks reserved specifically for greenies. But he never whined. Brother Lawrence's biographer wrote:

> Although his superiors assigned Lawrence to the most abject duties, he never let any complaint escape his lips. On the contrary, the grace that refuses to be disheartened by harshness and severity always sustained him in the most unpleasant and annoying assignments. Whatever repugnance he may have felt from his nature, he nevertheless accepted his assignments with pleasure, esteeming himself to be too happy either to suffer or to be humiliated by following the example of the Savior.

What a sycophant.

But I am going to have to delve deeper than my initial impressions, because Brother Lawrence apparently holds the keys to mindfulness in the Christian tradition. Apart from me, everybody adores him. Here's what Hannah Whitall Smith, a Quaker, said in the nineteenth century about Brother Lawrence's spiritual approach: "It fits into the lives of all human beings, let them be rich or poor, learned or unlearned, wise or simple. The woman at her wash-tub, or the stonebreaker on the road, can carry on the 'practice' here taught with as much ease and as much assurance of success as the priest at his altar or the missionary in his field of work." This sounds promising.

It occurs to me that it's no coincidence that Brother Lawrence's writing, neglected by French Catholics after his death, was subsequently championed by English and American radical Protestants like Hannah Smith: his DIY spirituality coordinated precisely with their worldview. No intermediary was necessary. Just step right in, folks! Scrub those dishes, and presto change-o, you're that much closer to God. Anyone can do it, anywhere, even in the most profane of spaces. You don't need a priest, a scribe, or a Eucharist. You just need a cutting board and a cleaver, and suddenly you're flying down the Spirituality Express.

RINSE, LATHER, REPEAT

For all my early doubts about Brother Lawrence, cooking does seem a marvelous way into spirituality, especially just after my month of fasting and self-denial. I enjoy cooking, although like most people I sometimes get tired of it. Maybe even Brother Lawrence in his less holy moments would have preferred to book a table at a Parisian bistro rather than knead the bread dough one more time. But although I too often have to cook hurriedly, there is something deeply healing about taking whole fresh ingredients that are inedible in their original state and transforming them into something delicious and nutritious. When I am anxious, the act of cooking or baking can settle me into a rhythm of tranquility.

I understand that's not true for everyone. I'm fascinated by how many Americans seem to have the all-singing, all-dancing kitchen but rarely cook in it. They eat out and order in, but don't actually produce much on their coveted stainless steel Wolf ranges. When I watch HGTV programs like *House Hunters*, I'm struck by the number of home shoppers who imagine that they will start cooking one day, but only when they have a gleaming, spacious kitchen like the one in house number three, whose center island could double as a helicopter landing pad.

If I feel superior on this point, it's because cooking is one of the only household chores I look forward to. But the sticking point with Brother Lawrence is that it's not just cooking where we're supposed to find God; it's in *any* menial task. I'm surprised to learn that Brother Lawrence confessed to his abbot that he had a "natural aversion" to kitchen work. In my mind I had pictured him as one of those James Beard types who realized his culinary calling in childhood. Brother Lawrence was French, after all. Apparently they do food rather well there. But no, it was not the actual creation of a meal that was special to him. Nowhere in the book does he or his biographer talk about Lawrence's love for cooking or his gravitation toward the comforting smells of stew and bread; in fact, considering how famous Lawrence is for being the great sacralizer of culinary chores, there's very little in here about the manual labor for which he was most famous.

Instead, his only thought was "about doing little things for the love of God, since he was not capable of doing great things." Brother Lawrence sought God in everyday tasks, which became for him conduits to the divine. Cooking, cleaning, shopping, cobbling shoes—the task itself was immaterial. What matters to God, Lawrence taught, is the love we express while doing it.

A dairymaid can milk cows to the glory of God.
—MARTIN LUTHER

So I am going to have to get out of my comfort zone and do more than flip a few pancakes for the Almighty. Where to begin? I start making a list of the household tasks I do every day, every week, and less regularly. As I do this, I'm astounded to see how much of my life is spent simply maintaining the status quo. Most days I cook, wash dishes, and pick up the house; every week I do the laundry, vacuum, pay the bills, go to the grocery store, and take care of our forlorn houseplants, among other things. Phil helps with some of these chores and has many of his own, but since he's gone ten hours every weekday and I generally work from home, the bulk of the regular maintenance falls to me.

The trick this month will be to find some redemptive spiritual value in all those menial tasks. I tend to focus on the end result of any chore, getting it over with to enjoy a clean(er) kitchen floor. I'm not a fan of the process itself, which seems like something to grin and bear. It's hard to get excited about the process when it simply repeats itself over and over: all of these are things I had to do yesterday or last week, and all are things I'll need to do again tomorrow or next week.

The round of regular daily chores doesn't even take into account the reality of how often things fall apart. Right now, Phil and I ought to find someone to upgrade our chimney, which has no cap. Although I've forbidden Phil from getting on the roof, he takes care of most of the other entropy as things break down in the house and the yard. Luckily for me—at least most of the time—he is a classic DIYer, the kind who would gladly perform his own vasectomy using a Time-Life home surgery manual if he could save a buck. He fixes computers, lays tile, hangs drywall, repairs cars, and stitches up ailing beanie babies who've lost their stuffing. His basement "man cave" has a sewing machine always at the ready, because really, what man cave would be complete without a sewing machine?

When our daughter was small, Phil's job required a good deal of travel, and it was inevitable that on the first day of a ten-day trip to

Japan or Italy or someplace equally inaccessible, an appliance would break down at home. It was astonishing how reliably this disaster would recur. He went to Germany, and the dishwasher started spewing soapy water on the kitchen floor. He flew to France for a long weekend—hey, it was a *very* difficult job—and suddenly there was no computer connection and the car wouldn't start.

After about two years of this I finally commented to him how exasperating it was that every appliance conspired to make my life miserable each time he removed his passport from its file. Then he explained something I honestly had not noticed: things were actually breaking down *all the time,* not just when he headed out the door. He hadn't seen the need to worry me about most of them, so he quietly went about fixing them, sometimes after I'd already gone to bed, like an oversized elf engineer.

GOD IN AN APRON

God is like that, repairing the world all the time. Even though it's hard for me to see the spiritual value in menial household chores, there's something deeply Christian about them. In a brilliant book about the theology of housekeeping, Margaret Kim Peterson says that it's precisely the never-ending nature of household tasks such as cooking that makes them "so akin to the providential work of God." Every day, every person in the household needs to be fed—*again.* We feed them with the knowledge that tomorrow morning, they will wake up hungry and we'll have to repeat the whole cycle.

Peterson says that our constant round of housework and God's initial act of creation have something in common: both are about bringing order from chaos. But God doesn't just put our earthly home into motion and let things take their course; he's constantly playing housekeeper. We see this in the Bible. When Adam and Eve are exiled from the garden and have to strike out on their own, God's first act is to clothe them. He gives the kvetching Israelites manna from heaven to snack on during their forty-year nature hike. He also becomes increasingly domesticated throughout the Old Testament, dwelling first in an ark, then a tabernacle, and finally a temple—a great biblical example of trading up, real estate wise, from a mobile home to a mansion.

God's son, Jesus, is also concerned with daily life and domestic cares, even though he cautions us not to be too anxious about them and chides his friend Martha when she freaks out about household duties. Jesus says that anyone who clothes the naked and feeds the hungry is also doing these same services for him—an interesting reproof to anyone who's apt to dismiss cooking and shopping as meaningless tasks. He compares the kingdom to a banquet and suggests that God wants every seat at the feast to be occupied; he teaches his disciples to pray to God for their daily bread, sanctifying that most basic human need. Even God's incarnation in Jesus might suggest something startling about the importance of housework: like housework, redemption is physical. God doesn't stand around watching humanity go to hell in a handbasket; he gets his own hands dirty by sending his Son to heave us from the muck. In Jesus, God is cleaning his house.

I'm fascinated by the way Peterson deals with the endless, repetitive nature of housework and how unsatisfying it can be, especially when we look at our homes and only see the tufts of dog hair adorning each corner, or the Tang-like orange band at the bottom of the shower liner. "All the more is this so when our homes are not all we might wish them to be. God's world is not as he wishes it to be, either," she writes. Touché.

With a new awareness, both painful and humorous, I begin to
understand why the saints were rarely married women.
—ANNE MORROW LINDBERGH

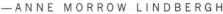

For Peterson, the importance in these repetitive chores is that they compose a litany of prayer. In church life, a litany is any kind of familiar, repeated prayer. In my husband's Episcopal liturgy, it's the communal prayer that alternates between the reader and the congregation. The reader petitions for the environment, for social justice, or for more far-reaching NPR reception, like any self-respecting liberal Episcopal church. The congregation occasionally proves that it is still awake by droning at prescribed intervals, "*Lordhearourprayer.*" That's a litany. The prayers change slightly, reflecting whether a congregant at the retirement home is sick or Minnie Olsworth had her C-section, but the responses, the timing, the basic structure are always the same. There is a comfortable familiarity in the routine.

According to Peterson, housework is precisely like this. A well-run household has a basic mealtime and some usual players, although the times and the diners may change depending on circumstance. The structure of the meal usually follows a prescribed path—salad, main course with side dish, and dessert if you don't have kids; chicken nuggets consumed only under threat of the absence of dessert if you do. And during it all—from the hour of preparation to the ten minutes of consumption and twenty minutes of cleanup before you all head out to piano lessons—there is the opportunity for prayer.

MINDFULNESS

In Brother Lawrence's world, as in mine, daily cooking was a given. The difference between us is that he saw cooking as an opportunity to become one with the Lord of the Universe, whereas I see it as the one snatch of my day when I can listen to *All Things Considered.* Cooking is allegedly the perfect hand-occupant during times of prayer because of its repetitive nature; the fact that I've made corn chowder so many times before means that I know the recipe by heart and can focus instead on God. Or at least that's the theory.

In practice I learn the very first week that this kind of spiritual multitasking feels artificial. I cook the meals, wash the entry hall floor—sullied by a film of rock salt and melted snow—and clean the house's one working bathroom. (The other is our ongoing renovation project, which is a spiritual discipline all in itself.) I do these chores in silence, but instead of enjoying the quiet as an accompaniment to my growing spiritual bliss, my mind zips around like the bamboo plants we keep trying to kill off in the backyard, which preserve themselves by sending off industrious, hardy shoots all the way to the other end of the lawn. My mind cannot stay present in the moment.

And that's when I at least attempt to be mindful of God and do chores; sometimes I skip out altogether. When my friend Alice mentions that she needs to clean her oven and is dreading it, I volunteer for the job before I quite know what I'm saying. She has a new baby and could use some help around the house. Since I've never actually cleaned an oven before, not once, I read up in *Home Comforts* about what's involved. It sounds like a boatload of hot, smelly work. How am I going to find God in this chore? Surely a quicker route to genuine religious experience would be to snort the spray cleaner and get high on the fumes.

Although I'm ashamed to admit it, nothing ever comes of my spontaneous offer to clean Alice's oven. I propose a date, but it doesn't work for her; I promise I'll get back to her and just . . . don't. When I next see her, she has either forgotten the offer or is too polite to mention my failure to follow through.

Although oven cleaning is a concrete practice, it's still unclear to me what it has to do with spiritual growth. This month's endeavor to "practice the presence of God" feels vague. What does that phrase even *mean*? I still have no idea what I'm supposed to be doing, and dear Brother Lawrence isn't exactly helping. I mine the book for details, trying to learn how he accomplished his perpetual feat of

Great peace is found in little busy-ness.
—GEOFFREY CHAUCER

Kitchen Zen. However, seventeenth-century hagiography is not the most appropriate genre for learning *how* Brother Lawrence cultivated his heightened spiritual state. The book's editor derives an inordinate amount of pleasure from describing how Lawrence suffered from gout, an ulcer, pleurisy, and other illnesses that refined his soul and fitted him for heaven, yada yada yada. But I'm not finding "The Five Steps Toward Oneness with God" that I'm hoping for. There's no checklist of things to do so I can follow in Lawrence's footsteps. It's only near the back of the book that I find this promising start to one of Lawrence's letters:

To the Reverend Mother N . . .

Since you have expressed such an eager desire to have me share with you the method I have used to arrive at that state of the presence of God in which our Lord by His mercy was willing to place me, I cannot conceal from you that it is with great reluctance that I allow myself to be won over by your persistence. I am writing only under any condition that you will not share my letter with anyone.

Well, bully for the Reverend Mother that she pushed him for some answers beyond his usual platitudes about "just practice God's presence every day," and also didn't take Lawrence's suggestion that she should burn the letter after reading. I like this lady.

This Reverend Mother continued to exchange letters with Lawrence despite her failing health, which should earn her kudos because Lawrence appears to have been an exasperating correspondent. I'm beyond irritated by his tendency to downplay her illness and obvious physical pain. "If we were quite used to practicing the presence of God, all sickness of the body would seem trivial to us," he lectures her. In other words, if your faith were only stronger, you'd be so holy you wouldn't notice the pain. Brother Lawrence's bedside manner gets worse: "I cannot understand how a soul who is with God and who wants only him is capable of suffering. My own experience proves this." So not only is the Reverend Mother's faith insufficient because she still endures some physical complaints, but Brother Lawrence's is perfect. The guy is now ticking me off.

So I stop reading his book and go rogue. One day when I'm alone in the house, I head into the kitchen to make cookie dough and begin simply talking to Jesus.

"You know, you don't have to give me the silent treatment," I challenge him. "Throw me a bone here!"

I'm not sure why I pick Jesus rather than God; Brother Lawrence hardly speaks of Jesus at all. But Jesus seems less abstract, more accessible. I like the idea of him pulling up a barstool to the laminate countertop and listening to me prattle on about my day. His head would be cocked slightly to the right, an eyebrow occasionally raised in interest. He would gratefully eat a sample of cookie dough, because the Son of Man doesn't have to worry about getting salmonella from raw eggs. He would mostly listen, asking the occasional probing question. He would lead me gently toward loving action without pointing out the inadequacies of my personal faith, as Brother Lawrence seems wont to do.

So I talk to Jesus. I confide aloud my anxieties about a family member, and unload about a problem at work. Girlfriend stuff. I don't tell Jesus how amazing he is, or do anything remotely worshipful. The experience is wholly self-centered, which is probably why it's the only time I've succeeded in staying in the present moment the entire month.

For prayer is nothing more than being on terms of friendship with God.

—TERESA OF AVILA

After a few days of this, the mindfulness practice gets a tad easier. "We must not be surprised at failing frequently in the beginning," Lawrence advises. That's an understatement. It's a good thing that I'm talking out loud to Jesus, because my mind is still like a sieve. It isn't until nearly the end of the month, after I've gotten more used to chatting up the Son in my kitchen, that I consult Brother Lawrence again and read the advice he gave to an admirer who wrote to him sometimes. He admonished her never to pray aloud: "Long speeches often become an occasion for straying." Jeepers, I just can't win. The one variation on mindfulness practice that has proven helpful is something Brother Lawrence IDs as a failure. Whatever.

FAILED SAINTS

Even though I find Brother Lawrence annoying in practice, I admit his spirituality is appealing in the abstract. There's something very American (and un-French) about assigning such godly and redemptive attributes to daily work. Lawrence, I am realizing, could be the patron saint of the 1950s American housewife, if he only wielded a Sunbeam blender and donned a chintz apron over his cassock.

Except that Brother Lawrence was never made a saint. I don't realize this until nearly the close of my unsuccessful month of mindfulness, and this piece of information increases my sympathy for him. I may not like him much myself, but my heart leaps up in loyalty to defend the guy. Not an official saint! This is a serious oversight that I mean to bring to the attention of the pope just as soon as I am retired and have time to pontificate via complaint letters. There are more than 2,500 entries in *Butler's Encyclopedia of Saints*, and some of them sound downright lame. I mean, for every St. George slaying a dragon and Perpetua getting bloodied in the lion's den, there are no-names like Frumentias of Ethiopia. Excuse me, *Frumentias*? And then there are the saints that are positively certifiable, like Christina the Astonishing, who was apparently astonishing in that she was flat-out weird. She could not tolerate the stench of other human beings (which was understandable—this was the Middle Ages after all), and basically terrorized the village as that crazy homeless woman who yells at everyone passing by. If Christina gets saintly props for being an early candidate for Bellevue, why not sweet Brother Lawrence?

"It isn't fair," I vent to my colleague Anna, who is sort of Catholic. (I say "sort of" because she grew up Catholic, never goes to church anymore, and has little good to say about it herself, but if she catches other people talking smack about the Holy See, she jumps on them with the fervor of a new convert.) "Brother Lawrence cleaned up after all those monks for years and did their grocery shopping and even fashioned their shoes. Why do all these other turkeys get to be saints and not him? He peeled their potatoes and took care of them when they were sick!" Okay, I don't actually know about that last part, but maybe he nurtured the sick when he wasn't telling them their illness was their own fault.

"What were his miracles?" she asks with some interest.

"His miracles? Um, I'm not sure. Isn't feeding a whole monastery for years on nothing but a kitchen garden kind of a miracle?"

Anna is unimpressed. "Well, if that's a miracle, then my grandma should be canonized too. She raised eight kids with no money and an alcoholic husband, and those kids all went to college."

"But Brother Lawrence should have been a saint. He served people for all those years without complaining. And in the end, there was nothing to show for it. He didn't even write his book himself—

somebody spoke a eulogy at his funeral, and somebody else gathered those thoughts together and published them. If they hadn't done that, and collected his letters, we wouldn't know anything at all about Brother Lawrence; he'd be totally lost to history."

"Projecting much?" she asks me wryly.

That comment hits home. It suddenly strikes me why I'm so sensitive about Brother Lawrence's lack of official saintly creds: He's an underappreciated housewife, the one everyone takes for granted. He's . . . a bit like me, and like a whole lot of people I know, primarily women. Anna's grandmother. My own grandmother.

So even though I've failed at his spiritual practice and can't stop criticizing his holier-than-thou attitude, I'm thankful to have met Brother Lawrence, and glad that there is a not-quite-saint in the canon of also-rans who focused on elevating the daily chores that take up so much of my life and energy.

At the end of the month, though, I don't feel any better off spiritually than I did at the beginning. At least with the fasting, I improved with my basic ability to accomplish the practice, even if I didn't have any profound spiritual awakenings. With Brother Lawrence and mindfulness, I feel I've missed the mark. I've experienced no spiritual epiphanies, no moments of transcendence while mindfully loading the dishwasher. Other than a few helpful (if one-sided) conversations with Jesus, this month has been a wash from a spiritual point of view.

There is one bright spot: my mind and heart may be the worst-trained in Christendom, but at least my house is almost unrecognizably clean. That's got to count for something.

lectio divination

The Bible is a most comforting book; it is also a most discomfiting book. Eat this book; it will be sweet as honey in your mouth; but it will also be bitter to your stomach. You can't reduce this book to what you can handle; you can't domesticate this book to what you are comfortable with. You can't make it your toy poodle, trained to respond to your commands.

—EUGENE PETERSON

As April dawns I'm relieved to put behind me the nebulous, guilt-inducing "practice of the presence of God" in favor of something more concrete. This month brings a spiritual practice I can sink my teeth into, one about which entire books have been written. How-to guides. With concrete steps. I think I'll be in better hands than I was with Brother Lawrence.

I'm trying out *lectio divina* (LEX-ee-oh de-VEEN-ah), an ancient spiritual practice that prescribes a way of discernment through reading and prayer. It's not about praying for things so much as it is about *becoming one* with God's will. That kind of union sounds a little too Brother Lawrence-y for my taste, but I look forward to the reading part. *Lectio divina* teachers want me to read deeply in the Bible, to cherish its people and stories. In other words, they want me to read the Bible as diligently as I have been known to study Harry Potter.

HOLY READING

I've always been a reader, thanks to my family. When I was three and my brother John was five, he taught me how to read. This is what my mother claims happened, anyway. That story has the whiff of the apocryphal to me, since I don't remember it at all. However the instruction occurred, by the second day of kindergarten the principal realized I was already reading fluently and understanding difficult words, so she zoomed me ahead to first grade. I was happy to make the switch, though I missed snack time and never met the mysterious Letter People my peers discussed on the playground.

Reading became a creative and intellectual outlet throughout childhood, as well as a refuge when times got bad in my family in my teens. The public library was like my church, a library card the equivalent of a passport to other places, even other worlds. As an adult I tend to inhale books, especially novels, tearing through from start to finish. I suspect, though, that this devouring approach is not going to cut it with the *lectio divina* teachers. *Lectio divina* is like your mother telling you not to bolt your food; it's about slowing down, chewing methodically, absorbing nutrients. Yet we are often impatient with this kind of reading. Oprah Winfrey once complained to novelist Toni Morrison that she would often have to go back over the same sentence several times to truly understand it. "That, my dear, is called *reading*," Morrison responded.

To help me learn how to practice *lectio divina*, I've enlisted two expert sources. Eugene Peterson opens his book on spiritual reading with an analogy of us reading Scripture like a dog might gnaw a bone. His dog is joyful to have the bone; for a time he plays with it and enjoys having others interact with it. Then he settles in to chew it in a more private area, turning it over for a long time, then burying it only to retrieve it again later and pick up where he left off. Peterson says that in Hebrew, the word we tamely translate as "meditate" on the Scriptures actually means "growl," like an animal growls over its prey. God wants us to growl in triumph over the Bible before settling in to wrestle with it and worry it like a bone. It's a marvelous image.

Peterson's overriding metaphor for *lectio* is also one I love: he draws upon a story from the nutty book of Revelation about how an angel came to John to impart a scroll of the Bible. John asked the angel to give him the scroll; the angel responded instead that John should eat it. Peterson says this is how Christians have to be with the Bible: we have to ingest it entirely, to let it bring oxygen to our veins and seep into our nerve endings. It is breakfast, lunch, and dinner.

I am madly enjoying Peterson's book, but there's little in it about how to *do lectio divina*, unless you take that whole swallow-the-scroll metaphor literally, which the surgeon general does not recommend. So in addition to *Eat This Book*, this month I'm also consulting more of a how-to guide called *Sacred Reading* by Michael Casey, an Australian monk. Casey follows ancient practice and breaks up *lectio divina* into four seemingly manageable steps:

1. *Lectio*: reading the text.
2. *Meditatio*: meditating the text. I learned last month while practicing the presence of God that meditation is hardly my strong suit, but I'm determined to keep an open mind.
3. *Oratio*: praying the text. We're supposed to ask God what it means for our lives.
4. *Contemplatio*: contemplating and living the text.

These last three steps blur together, but I hope the process will become clearer as I go along. Both Casey and Peterson make the point that the "steps" aren't necessarily linear; you don't start with the first and march purposefully through the fourth in chronological order.

You constantly spiral back, make new connections, skip around, or repeat something you didn't understand.

L E C T I O

Before I dive in to *lectio divina* and relearn how to read, I need to decide *what* to read. Casey recommends taking an entire book—a book of the Bible, a Christian classic, a commentary—and reading the whole thing, slowly, using *lectio divina*. I've chosen to focus on the Gospel of Mark, and I've decided to "read" it both in print and on audio. Centuries ago in the monastery, there would often be only

No man ever believes that the Bible means what it says: He is always convinced that it says what he means.
—GEORGE BERNARD SHAW

one copy of a Gospel or sacred text, so the monks would read it aloud slowly to each other. It seems like an excellent practice to me, so I'm using a set of CDs called *The Bible Experience*, a beautiful and powerful dramatization of the entire Bible with an African-American cast, to supplement my dog-eaten (literally) print copy of the NRSV.

Aside from its drama and beauty, I'm choosing to read all of Mark because I don't much care for the selectivity of other approaches to reading the Bible. I'm stubborn about the canon. I don't want to turn *Eat This Book* into *Eat This, Not That*, picking and choosing only the loveliest passages that fit with my existing understanding of faith. One of the *lectio divina* guides I consult has a "greatest hits" approach to help people get started with sacred reading, with a list of several hundred prayable Scriptures at the back. These are pretty much what you'd expect, and include some of the most beloved passages of the Bible: 1 Corinthians 13 on love, the Twenty-Third Psalm, and Jesus forgiving his killers from the cross. It's powerful stuff, but what about the rest of the Bible? Leviticus 21 has a verse about dwarves, hunchbacks, and blind people not being welcome in the kingdom of God, which is a troubling message in our more inclusive era; the book of Samuel has a funky story about David earning his chops as a tribal leader by collecting Philistine foreskins to present to his would-be bride. I'm not finding these passages anywhere in the *lectio divina* textbooks. On second thought, it would be hard to sustain serious prayer about harvesting foreskins. Maybe these *lectio divina* types do know what they're doing in selecting the most spiritual passages for deep prayer. But at the very least, I'm going to take Casey's suggestion and do the *whole* of Mark. Luckily for me, it's the shortest Gospel, and I believe it's foreskin-free.

Lectio divina advocates suggest that you find a quiet place to start this practice, sitting down with the text and reading aloud slowly to yourself. Instead of this, I take our dog, Onyx, for a walk. I've got my headphones blasting the Gospel of Mark for an initial read-through as I stride west past coffeehouses and restaurants. I want to get the big picture before narrowing down to the details.

I'm struck by the way Mark dives right into the story of Jesus. Not for him the introductory begats, the annunciation to Mary, the cozy nativity scene. Mark's pilot episode is fast-paced, with the adult Jesus' baptism, a brief introduction of the supporting cast, some exciting exorcisms and healings, an offstage forty-day temptation, and a montage of a preaching tour. Mark would have been a sought-after action writer in Hollywood. Everything happens "immediately" and "at once." His Gospel is plot driven. A half-hour walk up through the observatory grounds gets me about halfway through Mark's Gospel, which is rapid progress for this chilly April morning.

I continue listening a few times a week until I've heard the Gospel several times. Sometimes I zone out or become distracted by random thoughts (say, what's the difference between a jonquil, a crocus, and a daffodil?), but small details keep pulling me back into the text. For example, Jesus resurrects a twelve-year-old girl at the same time he heals a woman who has been bleeding for twelve years; a few chapters later there are twelve baskets of food left over after he miraculously feeds the five thousand—a miracle the twelve disciples can't quite wrap their heads around. And I wonder: what is the significance of the number twelve?

Lectio is the first step in *lectio divina*, so this kind of observation is a strong start. However, it feels like an academic exercise—interesting, but hardly life-changing. What's missing is that I'm not praying for inspiration. I'm supposed to approach the text *expecting to be changed*, not just hoping to someday dominate a Jeopardy category about Jesus trivia. I can't keep relating to the Bible with just my head. I'll have to find where it's speaking to my heart.

MEDITATIO: THE ANGRY JESUS

"Mom, is Jesus mad about something?" Jerusha asks. We're riding in the car on the way to an appointment, and I've left a CD of the Gospel of Mark in the disc player from when I was running errands earlier.

At this moment on the CD, Jesus sounds apoplectic. He's railing about how we honor him with our lips while inwardly we are the worst kind of hypocrites. "Sexual immorality! Theft! Murder!" he cries.

I stare straight ahead but sense Jerusha becoming uncomfortable with this new side of Jesus. *This* is not the sweet shepherd she met at Sunday School. Jesus barrels on: "Adultery! Greed! Slander! Pride! Envy! Folly!" I hastily silence him with the press of a button.

Jesus' rage makes me uncomfortable too. In the second stage of *lectio divina*, once we've gotten past a literal understanding, we're supposed to dig for the meaning, and hopefully find Christ in each passage. The divine Christ is here in Mark, certainly, but the human Jesus is melting down a surprising number of times. It's not just the Pharisees and the scribes that tick him off; it's his own disciples. They're stand-ins for us, always demanding a sign, not understanding about the miracles, too frequently wanting concrete explanations for mystery.

> *Most people are bothered by those passages of Scripture*
> *they do not understand, but the passages that*
> *bother me are those I do understand.*
> —MARK TWAIN

The disciples don't realize who Jesus is (though interestingly enough, the demons comprehend right away). His followers are jockeying for position, and they don't understand why Jesus has to suffer—or, perhaps more to the point, why *they* have to suffer. Jesus wants them to understand about suffering and death. They want to fast-forward to the good parts, arguing about which of them will be most prestigious in heaven.

When I follow up the audio listening with a print read-through of the Gospel of Mark, I realize that hardly a page goes by in the entire Gospel when the disciples aren't misunderstanding something—and Jesus doesn't always bear their incomprehension with Christlike patience. Why have I never noticed before how angry he is? In chapter 8, after the miraculous feeding of the five thousand and the four thousand, the disciples have a hissy fit because there's no bread. No bread! Jesus responds like an exasperated parent who has repeated the same lesson 1,547 times and can't believe the kids still don't grasp the point. "Why are you talking about having no bread?" Jesus demands. "Do you still not perceive or understand? Are your hearts hardened?

Do you have eyes, and fail to see? Do you have ears, and fail to hear? And do you not remember?"

In other words, *What kind of idiots are you people, anyway?!*

This is the kind of passage that I often skip over or, if I read it at all, want to ascribe to others: the clueless, bumbling disciples in their day, or the people I disagree with in my own. They are the "other." But the audio version has a power and proximity that my usual skim of the same material doesn't impart. This isn't about the disciples; it's about me. It's one thing to read a nice, tidy print Bible in which Jesus chastises his followers with words in brilliant red. It's quite different when Jesus is shouting, "You hypocrite!" in your very own ear. The lack of safe distance is palpable.

And don't even get me started on how angry he sounds at the money-changers in the temple in chapter 11. Panting, screaming. The fury I hear in Jesus' usually well-modulated voice seems meant just for me. *I* have made his temple a den for robbers. *I* have let him down. Listening to Mark's Gospel feels like an über-intense therapy session, with accusations flying and disappointments made plain.

Lectio divina, I'm finding, is hard-hittingly personal. I'm starting to understand why Peterson calls it "a way of reading that guards against depersonalizing the text into an affair of questions and answers, definitions and dogmas." I also see why, in the book of Revelation, the angel warns John that when he eats the scroll it will taste as sweet as honey on his tongue but then turn to bitterness in his stomach. Peterson says the point is that we like the *idea* of the Bible and often find it sweet at first introduction. Then, as we begin to dig, it becomes increasingly less comfortable.

Not only am I less comfortable, but the Bible is giving me indigestion.

The Bible isn't really at all good at being an instruction manual.
It's good at leading us into a tangle of wild poetry, heartbreaking
stories, contradictions, twists and turns, the concrete struggles of
a vast array of unruly, disparate human beings being sought
after by God. . . . The Bible isn't a cage that contains God,
making God available to take out or hang in our living room,
it's a witness to the fecund, ungraspable Other
(and our relationship to that Other).

—DEBBIE BLUE

ORATIO: LECTIO DIVINATION

When the Bible makes us uncomfortable, as Jesus' anger is doing, it's time to pray. *Ora* is Latin for "prayer," the third of my four steps. Strange as it sounds, *oratio* is the stage of *lectio divina* where I hit a wall—not because I don't believe in prayer, but because in the past I may have believed in it too much.

Call it lectio divination: expecting the Bible to cough up a sought-after insight every time you open it. In the *oratio* stage of *lectio divina*, we're encouraged to engage the text and come at it with questions: *What does this mean for me? How does this passage relate to my life? What does God want me to do?* But the danger is in assuming that a particular passage was preordained to answer the question of the moment, like a divining rod pointing straight to lifesaving water.

I wish things did work that way, that the Bible were more of an answer guide than a pastiche of enigmatic tales. Occasionally prayer and Scripture do appear to work this way together. When I was in my mid-thirties, I went on a retreat at the Abbey of Gethsemani to write and also to pray about a strong spiritual impression I'd had some weeks earlier, suggesting that Phil and I were supposed to have a second child. To be honest, the suggested "impression" had been very specific: there was a son who wanted to join our family, and he loved music. Phil and I worried the question of a second baby endlessly. The timing was not great; Phil was getting his doctorate, and we had the worst health insurance in the Western world. ("So you lost a finger. Big deal! You still have nine others.")

Before I left on the retreat, I prayed that God would use the time to show me what we were to do. And there, at every turn, were what seemed to be clear answers to my prayer: in the chanting, we sang a psalm about how the person with many children is blessed with a quiverful of arrows. In fact, we actually sang it twice because of a rare screwup in the service order that had us repeating the same psalm twice in one day. This seemed like a profound confirmation, a sign that God had heard my prayer and was speaking to me through the time-honored language of the Bible's oldest music. That, coupled with the ubiquitous images of the Madonna and her infant, gave my heart confidence that a second child was the right path to take. These were signs from God!

Except that it hasn't quite worked out that way, because said child did not materialize. When I had that sense of Scripture being an answer to my prayer, other parts of our story simply did not occur to me, the parts where the dream is deferred or destroyed by unexpected infertility and miscarriage. Those parts of the story unfolded over time, amid sorrow and frustration and yes, even shame. It's now years later, and I am left wondering whether I overspiritualized a coincidence. Was the psalm that we prayed at Gethsemani—not once but twice in the time I was there—merely an accident? Math is not on my side here. I mean, if the monks pray through the entire Psalter every two weeks and I was there for three and a half days, the odds aren't really one in a million. In fact, they increase to about 50 in 150, odds that hardly require miraculous intervention.

This long-standing disappointment jostles itself to the forefront of my mind as I approach *lectio divina*. I try to stake down the temptation to regard any wisdom gained from merely opening the Bible and pointing to the first passage I see as divine. But what am I to think one day in April when, overwhelmed by responsibilities and tax anxieties, I open my threadbare print Bible straight to this passage from the Gospel?

Take heart, it is I; do not be afraid. (Mk. 6:50)

I feel immediately comforted. Somebody up there likes me. There's someone in my corner. Coincidence, coincischmence! Yes, a skeptic would say that this particular fortune cookie had about a 99 percent chance of hitting its target; when am I *not* anxious and fearful about something? Yet I choose to believe that God sees and hears, that God loves me and does not want me to be consumed with worry. I don't wish to inhabit an entirely rational world with no mystery. *Lectio divina* is going to be heart and head, not just head.

CONTEMPLATIO: THE ELUSIVE POT OF GOLD

Michael Casey makes the point in *Sacred Reading* that the four stages of *lectio divina* aren't clearly delineated but function more like the shimmering hues of a rainbow, ebbing and flowing and sometimes overlapping. It's a lovely image, but one thing is clear from his book: the pot of gold at the end of the rainbow is supposed to be *contemplatio*.

The word *contemplatio* is where we get "contemplation," but the Latin implies far more than sitting around with our chins in our hands, thinking. It's a course of action, moving forward from the text. The Bible is supposed to bear fruit in our lives; as I'm seeing in the Gospel of Mark, when the sower scatters his seed along the path, you want to be the "good seed" that sprouts sturdy plants, not the seed that gets choked by weeds, scorched by the sun, or felled by shallow roots.

The human qualities of the raw materials show through. Naivety, error, contradiction, even (as in the cursing Psalms) wickedness are not removed. The total result is not "the Word of God" in the sense that every passage in itself, gives impeccable science or history. It carries the Word of God.
—C. S. LEWIS

I get the concept, and I don't want to be a bad seed. However, I'm not feeling much mystical union with the divine. At all. This is where it becomes very clear that, like with fasting in February, a month is not long enough to make any real headway with a new spiritual practice. Both Peterson and Casey talk about the years that are necessary to make tangible progress with *lectio divina*. Years! "Lifelong exposure to God's word is more like a marathon than a sprint," Casey cautions. I'm more interested in merely jogging once around the block.

But if I'm going to fail, I'd like to at least learn something in the process, and *lectio divina* has been surprisingly helpful in that regard. Primarily, it has shown me how I tend to skim the surface, not only of the Bible but of the Christian faith itself. Casey says that one "benefit that comes with the regular reading of the Bible is that we are brought face to face with the superficiality of our existing commitment. It is easy to believe that our lives are inspired by the Gospels if we keep the Gospels at a distance." Confronting the Gospel of Mark each day has made me realize how demanding the Christian faith is, despite all my attempts to make light of it. Jesus' disquieting temper tantrums illuminate my hard-heartedness; and the Bible, with its alternating impenetrability and bluntness, brings my own weaknesses into sharp relief.

I've now failed, to one degree or another, at three different spiritual practices, which is demoralizing. I'm disappointed in myself, but somehow I don't think that God is. Even though reading the Gospel of Mark has shown me many of the ways I fall short, the Bible has been valuable in cracking the pedestal of "real" Christian faith for me. Perhaps I get so disturbed by Jesus' anger and humanity because I am so afraid of those very shadows within myself. Maybe my determination to explore the Bible, warts and all, and to undertake the whole of the canon, exposes an underlying yearning for God to accept *me*, warts and all. I don't want to put forward only my acceptable bits for prayer, don my Sunday best to inhabit a relationship with God. He gets to work with me in my sweat pants, as I kick up my feet on the couch. He gets to love me through my selfish, disciple-like desires to gain prestige or avoid suffering. Maybe he'll love me by shouting at me to try harder, and this time I will listen.

Near the end of the month I have a minor epiphany. I'm walking Onyx and listening to Mark 13, in which Jesus speaks of the master returning suddenly in the night. His servants are supposed to stay on their toes while the master is gone so they can be prepared for his return, even though they don't know precisely when that will happen. Onyx and I are well into the woods today, up in the winding trails of Ault Park while I listen to the Gospel. Just after Jesus admonishes his hearers to "keep watch" because they don't know the day or hour of his coming, everything goes silent. There is no more sound from the audio Bible.

I suddenly become aware of how alone Onyx and I are, there in the trees with their new foliage, surrounded by the trill of birds and the high-pitched buzz of insects. A woodpecker thwacks away in the distance as Onyx lifts a leg to distribute largesse at his 437th tree. *Keep watch*, I think. Am I awake?

I wonder if the audio has included that moment of silence intentionally, to jolt listeners out of their comfort zones, if only for a moment. The thief in the night has come: a moment of sudden losses.

Then I realize I have a faulty headphone jack, which has dislodged during the hike. Only technical difficulties, then. Still, the experience of sudden disconnection from Jesus has been unsettling. I'm hardly at the stage where I'm experiencing mystical union with the divine, but I can honestly say I've been hanging on his every word.

nixing shoppertainment

The wonderful thing about simplicity is its ability to give us contentment. Do you understand what a freedom this is? To live in contentment means we can opt out of the status race and the maddening pace that is its necessary partner. We can shout "No!" to the insanity which chants, "More, more, more!" We can rest contented in the gracious provision of God.

—RICHARD FOSTER

I'm not much of a shopper. My Midwestern frugality is so ingrained that I just can't override certain price ceilings I have in my mind. A purse should cost no more than thirty dollars, for example, and a woman should only have one purse at a time or she will lose her keys and wallet. Or at least, *I* will lose my keys and wallet. I am entirely monogamous with purses; I am faithful to one at a time until the day my laptop computer has worn the straps off it, which usually takes about three years. Then I brave the stores to find a new workhorse purse, sometimes aided by a friend like my buddy Donna, the Augustine fan from chapter 1. She helped me shop for a new handbag a few years ago and was undaunted by my various rules. She actually seemed pleased at the prospect of a shopping challenge.

"It can't cost more than thirty dollars," I instructed. "It has to have long, sturdy straps, and be big enough to hold my laptop and at least one heavy hardback, but not be colossal enough to give me scoliosis. It has to be a solid color that will go with everything. It can't have been made by slave labor. Oh, and it has to have lots of little pockets inside."

"Oooo-kay!" she said. An experienced shopper, she took charge, and within an hour had found me the perfect candidate at a Filene's Basement in Manhattan. It was a splurge for me at $34.99, but it met all the requirements. We celebrated with cupcakes at Magnolia Bakery.

It was a marvelous day, being with Donna, but in general, I'm not a fan of shopping. The good news about this is that my May practice of not shopping should be a breeze. I already have a lifetime of stored memories of shoppertainment deprivation, and aside from a brief stint in junior high when I cared about details like designer labels, I'm not that fussed about fashion. What's more, I'm married to the biggest cheapskate in America, whose car has 200,000 miles on it and who wears his shoes until the sole is hanging from the leather and I can glimpse his socks. Phil comes by this honestly; he was born to a long line of cheapskates. When we all get together at Thanksgiving and for summer holidays, we unconsciously indulge in a little game I call Competitive Frugality. Conversations go something like this:

"Hey, I like that shirt on you. Is that new?"

"Well, new to me. I got it for three bucks at Goodwill."

"That's great. Hey, check out my new jeans. I dug them out of the dumpster *behind* Goodwill."

"Seriously? Score!"

I'm exaggerating, but not by much. The whole ethos of our family encourages thrift and making do with less. I own twelve pairs of shoes, which for an American female is downright ascetic. Not shopping is going to be so easy.

THINKING BIG

This month I'm going to abstain from all shopping except for our weekly groceries. Anything that's not immediately necessary—anything that's a want and not a need—will be put on hold. My first small test is on May 3, when I squeeze out the last remaining drop of foundation from my cosmetics tube. Going nearly a month without foundation is probably not what the saints meant when they talked about "dying to self," but it's a start. Makeup is not a need. I'm doing well so far with this spiritual practice.

> *Frugality is good if Liberality be join'd with it. The first is leaving off superfluous Expenses; the last bestowing them to the Benefit of others that need.*
>
> —WILLIAM PENN

I'm also going to avert my eyes from advertising. Since we have DVR, I'm accustomed to skipping over television commercials, but this month I'm trying to steer clear of print ads as well. Suddenly, they are everywhere: billboards on the Interstate, full-color spreads in the magazines I read, pop-up annoyances on websites. It's like playing Whac-A-Mole every day to avoid them, but I'm succeeding enough that I start to feel proud of myself.

I should know by now, in my fifth month of spiritual experimentation, that the moment I start patting myself on the back is the precise moment I begin to fail. My confidence erodes when I commence reading Richard Foster, my spiritual guru for the month. Apparently, rejecting consumer culture is just the tip of the iceberg. What I need to aim for is simplicity in every area of my life. In *Freedom of Simplicity: Finding Harmony in a Complex World*, Foster encourages me to look beyond the practice of rejecting consumer culture to get to the root of what simplicity means for Christians. Which is anything but simple. "There simply are no easy answers to the tough questions of how we are to relate with integrity to the modern world," Foster writes. Terrific.

But there are clues: I need to be hyperaware of all the ways I seek status and approval from other people. For many people, that's shopping, but it's no real feather in my cap that shopping's just not my thing. Even though I'm not defining my worth by the label on my jeans, I have my own vanity Waterloos. Like being petted with praise when I speak at a conference and people applaud my ideas, my brain, my verbal quickness, my humor. I just eat that shit up. And yes, I say "shit" here because that's what the potty-mouthed apostle Paul calls anything that we feel inordinately proud of but ultimately doesn't point to God. The word he uses in Philippians 3 is *skubula*, which is not the most respectable way Paul could have phrased it. The Greek of his day had its own euphemisms, polite terms like *poop* and *caca*. Paul could have chosen any of those words, but he didn't, presumably because he wanted to call attention to the foulness of all our status-seeking. We are sinners, full of shit. I most of all. There is excrement in me.

Foster wants me to analyze my whole life, not just my materialism, for anything that's pulling me away from a simple life with God. This requires keeping a log of all my daily activities. And I do mean all of them. If I spend twenty minutes watching YouTube videos of cats who've been trained to flush the toilet, something my ten-year-old finds inordinately entertaining, I'm supposed to write that down. If I clock an hour looking at catalogs—wait, I'm not allowed to do that this month—I have to record that too. After I've spilled everything into the list, I'm to rank the items into four categories:

- Absolutely essential (1)
- Important but not essential (2)

- Helpful but not necessary (3)
- Trivial (4)

I feel dorky doing this exercise throughout early May. It reminds me of the "mission statements" that a lot of my friends wanted to write in the 1990s, inspired by Steven R. Covey's *Seven Habits of Highly Effective People*. I basically failed at the whole mission statement thing, but I am going to give this list a genuine Girl Scout try.

I'm supposed to wait until the end of the month to add them all up, but I'm too impatient and take stock after about a week. I've assembled quite a list. The next part is the kicker: "ruthlessly eliminate all of the last two categories and 20 percent of the first two."

What! *Everything* from the last two categories? Is he serious?

Here's what is in my bottom two categories: all the fun stuff. Like going to see *Star Trek* in the theater with my family, or watching the Reds lose again, or staying up too late to laugh with friends at book club. All that's left when those frivolities disappear is the endless round of work tasks that wound up in the "essential" column: the final chapters I need to edit before I can transmit one of my author's books into production, the edits I need to make on my own book before I submit it to my publisher, the conference paper I have to conjure out of thin air by next week. This new life doesn't strike me as joyfully simple; it sounds dreary and austere. I get to go to work, and I get to floss my teeth. Blech.

OKAY, THINKING SMALLER NOW

This austerity doesn't resemble the joyfully simple life I am craving. It also doesn't sound much like a life Jesus would prescribe; after all, the guy's inaugural miracle occurred at a party where he turned water into wine. Jesus was hardly a killjoy.

I stop obsessively writing down all my activities. As much as I'm loving the Foster book—the best thing I've read so far for this sainthood project—I'm going to give myself a pass on the puritanical self-scrutiny of every single minute of my days. Maybe years from now when I am some kind of Super Christian I will feel ready to embrace the kind of monastic life he recommends. And it *is* monastic. The Benedictines used to say that life should be *ora et labora*—work and prayer. That's pretty much all that's left to me after cutting out inessential activities. And I only ranked prayer as essential because I thought I should, not because it *feels* essential in the way that catching up on the last-ever episodes of *Battlestar Galactica* feels essential. I do have my priorities.

So I return to the original focus of not shopping and deal with the glaring problem of Mother's Day. I kind of forgot about it until after May had already started, which is a problem because now I can't buy a gift. My mother loves getting special presents, and since my bohemian brother rarely remembers to do anything, I feel the whole Mother's Day burden on my shoulders. Do I skirt the letter of the law by telling my husband what to buy and having him place the order? Even I can see that's cheating. Do I send a card and promise a gift on, say, June 1? That might actually work.

I know what Brother Richard would say now: why am I trying to commodify the love and respect I feel for my mother by spending a fortune on flowers that will wilt, books she could check out of the library, and chocolate that will last approximately six minutes in her house? Mother's Day is a celebration of love, not presents. And part of the whole joy of the day is knowing that I have the kind of mom who will completely understand that I can't buy a gift right now because of some nutty book I'm researching. I call and explain. She is not just accepting but delighted, especially when I promise to come visit over Memorial Day weekend—the best substitute for a gift.

THE COMFORTABLE SPIRIT

A few years ago I took care of a friend after she had a face-lift, her fiftieth birthday present to herself. If I had ever harbored any interest in getting plastic surgery, that weekend with Margaret (not her real name) may well have cured it. The surgery itself was done on a Friday morning, and the clinic released her to my care in the early afternoon, after I helped her to get dressed and listened to the nurse's instructions about pain medication. I couldn't believe they were letting her go home in that condition. The parts of Margaret's face that I could see around the bandages were already turning shades of saffron and indigo. As I drove the car gingerly to her house, she dozed in the passenger seat, then mumbled for me to pull over so she could throw up by the roadside.

It was a mystery to me why Margaret wanted the surgery. She already looked years younger than her age, thanks to healthy living and a number of smaller procedures and Botox injections. She was one of the most beautiful women I knew, and frankly I was a little in awe of her. But she was never satisfied with her looks. I hoped that this major face-lift would be the last of her attempts to stave off the inevitable aging process, but I had my doubts.

> *There are two ways to get enough: one is to continue to accumulate more and more. The other is to desire less.*
> —G. K. CHESTERTON

That evening, I read a novel and puttered around Margaret's house while she slept off the anesthetic. How I loved her house. She had, as a single woman, been able to purchase a veritable mansion that had ties to one of the city's early entrepreneurs, a testament to Margaret's own financial success and to Cincinnati's reasonable real estate prices. It was a gorgeous house, with original woodwork, a well-appointed kitchen, a spacious formal dining room, and six bedrooms. Margaret had a flair for interior decoration, and every room bespoke her impeccable taste.

Yet she was always buying things. When we would get together, usually for lunch or to catch an artsy movie, the conversation often turned to some new purchase, often an extravagant one. She had an account at one of the city's finest furniture shops and was forever shopping for elegant dressers, rugs, and paintings. However, her joy in each new purchase was short-lived, and she often complained of problems with designers and tradesmen. The drapes, delivered at long last, were several inches too short; the custom-designed stained glass windows contained too much yellow, her least favorite color.

I never see Margaret anymore. We parted awkwardly after a quiet disagreement, and she never called me again. I still think about her often and I miss her company; she was funny, smart, and very interested in art and music. But her soul seemed unexpectedly discontented with her life and its cast of characters, always peering beyond her present situation to the next purchase, the next makeover. She was surrounded by beauty, but seemed incapable of appreciating it for long. She wanted—thought she needed—more.

Although it's hard to admit, I see a good deal of Margaret's restlessness in myself. I feel clear-sighted enough to diagnose and judge materialism in a former girlfriend, but wasn't I the one wandering around her house sighing with pleasure at all the pretty things? I was often envious of Margaret's house, books, art, and yes, her freedom as a single woman to do pretty much as she pleased. I'm no more ready than Margaret to implement Richard Foster's wise counsel about how real simplicity begins when we stop looking to the outside world to validate our existence:

Perhaps no work is more foundational to the individual embodying Christian simplicity in the world than our becoming comfortable in our own skin. The less comfortable we are with ourselves, the more we will look to things around us for comfort. The more assured we are with ourselves, the less assurance we will need from things outside us.

COVETING AND THE PROBLEM OF CHOICE

My secret longings for Margaret's beautiful house bring me to the crux of my spiritual practice this month: The problem isn't shopping. The secret problem is coveting.

My name is Jana and I am a coveter. I like fantasizing about trips I'll take all over the world, and I envy people who have the wherewithal to travel. I envy other women's svelte figures, even though I'm too lazy to do the exercise that could ever result in that physique. And I buy into a culture and an advertising industry that rest upon the bedrock notion that people can and should be made to want what they don't yet have. Not coveting would be downright un-American.

I decide to explore what the Bible has to say about coveting, discovering what I suspected: coveting is not exactly encouraged. In the Ten Commandments, the Bible calls attention to the "do not covet" commandment by repeating it. That's because in the Hebrew language, there's no easy way to signal emphasis. You can't italicize or underline anything, like you might in English, and there's no such thing as an exclamation point. You can't say, "God *really* wants you to keep *this commandment in particular!*" What you can do is repeat it, because in Hebrew, if it's worth saying once then it's worth saying seventeen times. So in the Bible, the last commandment is rendered "Thou shalt not covet, thou shalt not covet," and it's the only one of the Ten Commandments that merits double billing. Here's the text from Exodus 20:

> You shall not covet your neighbor's house; you shall not covet your neighbor's wife, or male or female slave, or ox, or donkey, or anything that belongs to your neighbor.

This month's spiritual practice of not shopping has led me to a deeper underlying issue: now I have to try not to covet. In fact, every

I have learned, in whatever state I am, to be content.
—THE APOSTLE PAUL (Philippians 4:11)

spiritual practice I've attempted so far has resulted in failure not because I didn't adhere to the basic requirements of each experiment—I didn't cheat on my fast or neglect to listen to the Gospel of Mark, for example—but because the practices started pointing me to more profound issues below the surface that I couldn't quite face. I kept the fast, but I realized midway through that I was fasting for the wrong reasons. I was as worldly and selfish on February 28 as I'd been on February 1. With *lectio divina*, I adhered to the letter of the law, but never allowed myself to be vulnerable to the Bible's claims on my life. Where I was once too quick to imagine the Bible's words as direct answers to my prayers, now I'm reluctant to trust the book again.

This month I'm determined to dig beyond the superficial practice of not shopping to the underlying, and much more difficult, practice of not coveting. When I have to order a book for work through Amazon—I need it for business, really!—I try to whiz past the site with blinders on, ignoring all of Amazon's well-timed recommendations for my weakest spots. *If you liked* Settlers of Catan, *you'd be sure to enjoy every other board game the company has ever made! If you bought a lawnmower on Amazon* [guilty], *you must need a weed whacker too!*

I wonder if coveting is worse in the twenty-first century since we're presented with an unprecedented number of choices. In 1949, the average American grocery store carried 3,750 items; today that number is near 45,000. Half a century ago, you might have walked to your little downtown bookstore to find a small selection of a couple thousand titles; today, there are twenty-four million books listed on Amazon.com.

According to some psychologists, all this choice comes at a cost. Sheena Iyengar's research on choice started when she was a graduate student and used to go to a big weekly market in the Bay Area. Despite the vastness of the market (250 types of cheese!) and her own gourmet tendencies, she hardly ever bought anything there. On a hunch, she decided to try an experiment that wound up becoming the basis for her career research and later the book *The Art of Choosing*: she set up a table at the market with samples of jam. When she offered six varieties of jam in a taste test, 30 percent of the customers who tried the jam went on to buy a jar or two. When she put twenty-four varieties on her sample table, she had more floor traffic of people stopping by for a taste, but far fewer actually made a purchase—only 3 percent went on to buy a jar of jam. The lesson Iyengar learned from this seemed counterintuitive: there is such a thing as too much choice. It turns out that we get overwhelmed easily.

It's not just in consumer behavior that we have a dizzying array of selections. We now enjoy unprecedented choice in how we arrange our families, space our children (or have them at all), decide on a major, or even find a religion. In past generations, our religious affiliation was mostly decided for us by our parents (if you're born a Lutheran, you are a Lutheran; pass the hot dish) or limited by simple geography. One of Iyengar's long-term experiments questions whether having more choice in matters of religion makes people happier. It doesn't. Surprisingly, the religions that claim the happiest people are those that make some of the decisions for you by removing certain choices; the unhappiest people belonged to the most open-minded and tolerant faiths. Reform Jews and Unitarians were the most susceptible to depression, while fundamentalists faced adversity with optimism and experienced greater hope. It turns out that limits are often very good things.

When I ponder this, the point of this month's practice hits me: it's not just about curbing materialism, though that's a good thing, or even about not coveting. It's about taking some choices out of the mix, of letting God's guidance dictate the basic contours of what I will and won't do. I'm not just reducing physical clutter by not shopping; I need to reduce spiritual clutter by becoming the kind of Christian who does not covet. I'm going to get off the *more, more, more* treadmill and set spiritual limits in order to cultivate simplicity. Eureka!

But shortly after this epiphany, here is the thought that hits me: *I really like that Richard Foster guy, and want to read all of his books. I can't wait for May to be over so I can buy them.*

~~Centering Prayer~~
er, ~~The Jesus Prayer~~
look! a squirrel!

A monk when he eats, drinks, sits, officiates, travels or does any other thing must continually cry: "Lord Jesus Christ, Son of God, have mercy on me!" so that the name of the Lord Jesus, descending into the depths of the heart, should subdue the serpent ruling over the inner pastures and bring life and salvation to the soul.

— *THE PHILOKALIA*

School's out, so why am I feeling so frazzled? The sudden absence of homework has made for a happier child and two parents on temporary furlough from their quarter-time jobs of sitting at the kitchen counter to supervise long division. My work is going well, except that there's too much of it. Multiple deadlines and a string of travel have left me exhausted, and an unexpected summer sinus infection, mild but annoying, plagues me as I go about my business. They're all minor complaints, and I even feel guilty for having them, but the end result is a run-down and irritable me.

"Enervated," I say to Phil one day. I am *enervated*. The term itself seems a cruel joke—a word that should be "energized" but took a sudden turn to the dark side to zap everybody's juices.

What might help, I hope, is this month's spiritual practice: contemplative prayer, about which I have long been curious. I'll start with Centering Prayer, which is one way of doing contemplative prayer. *Open Mind, Open Heart*, Thomas Keating's classic book on the subject, is my assigned reading for June. He spends a good deal of time on the notion that contemplative prayer has always been an integral part of Christian spirituality—the book's subtext being that Father Keating didn't just make it up one day. His early descriptions lure me to the practice: "Centering Prayer is a discipline designed to reduce the obstacles to contemplative prayer," he explains. "Its modest packaging appeals to the contemporary attraction for how-to methods." Sold! This sounds like the kind of guide I had hoped for from Brother Lawrence back in March. Father Keating wants me to take twenty minutes a day to sit in silence and open myself up to God. Surely even I can manage twenty minutes of contemplation.

Centering Prayer isn't like the kinds of prayer most Christians are used to, where we petition God for *things*, like good health or greater understanding. Or a new laptop—not that I'd know anything about praying for that. The practice focuses on being still, turning to what Keating calls "a fuller level of reality" that's always around us but that we often don't notice amidst the usual chaos of our lives. I'm in full agreement with the basic goal: that we stop yammering to God about our petty concerns and take the time to listen.

We need to shut up. *I* need to shut up.

Pause for a moment, you wretched weakling, and take stock of yourself: Who are you, and what have you deserved, to be called like this by our Lord?

—THE CLOUD OF UNKNOWING, 13th century

I'd like to use Keating's book to get started with Centering Prayer, but despite the early promise of a how-to approach, it quickly becomes too theoretical for my taste. Plus there is a weird section in a Q&A portion of the book where a reader asks Keating, "Does my guardian angel know what goes on in my Centering Prayer?" It's news to me that I even have a guardian angel, let alone one who'd be snooping in my deepest prayers, and the idea creeps me out. So after a good skim of the Keating book I put it aside in favor of Cynthia Bourgeault's more accessible and down-to-earth guide *Centering Prayer and Inner Awakening*, which my editor recommended.

Bourgeault begins by posing the question, "Why do we need yet another book on Centering Prayer?"

A: "Because Jana didn't understand the first one she read."

Well, Bourgeault doesn't say my name specifically, but she does politely hint that I'm not the only one who found the book by Thomas Keating—her own teacher, as it happens—too lofty. I'm heartened by the author's admission that it took her many years to fix on a contemplative prayer practice; she'd been an Episcopal priest for a decade already before she discovered Centering Prayer. Maybe I have a shot at this.

Here is what Bourgeault says about getting started:

> It's very, very simple. You sit, either in a chair or on a prayer stool or mat, and allow your heart to open toward that invisible but always present Origin of all that exists. Whenever a thought comes into your mind, you simply let that thought go and return to that open, silent attending to the depths. Not because thinking is bad, but because it pulls you back to the surface of yourself. You use a short word or phrase, known as a "sacred word," such as "abba" (Jesus' own word for God) or "peace" or "be still" to help you let go of the thought

promptly or cleanly. You do this practice for twenty minutes, a bit longer if you'd like, then you simply get up and move on with your life.

It sounds like a cinch, doesn't it? I appreciate the fact that Bourgeault opens with this section on how to *do* Centering Prayer, rather than merely what it is. I like the hands-on approach, and for the first few

Effortlessly, take up a word, the symbol of your intention to surrender to God's presence, and let the word be gently present.

—M. BASIL PENNINGTON

days I slowly read the book and try the practice for twenty minutes at lunchtime. But while Bourgeault's book is infinitely clearer to me than Keating's, in a way that makes it worse: I can see all too clearly now that I am going to fail. Here are some things that she tells us not to do when practicing Centering Prayer, all of which I am doing or have done:

- Don't assume that silence is something to be filled up. Don't think of God as a "content provider" who spills urgent messages into your addled brain the moment there is a little silent space for him to do so.
- Don't repeat your sacred word like a mantra. It's just a place-holder in case you need to refocus your attention. (Oh.)
- Don't evaluate how you're doing midstream as if this were a judged Olympic performance.
- Don't *resist* a thought, *retain* a thought, or *react to* a thought.
- Don't fall asleep.
- Don't listen, don't think, don't pray. (Wait . . . wasn't praying precisely the point?)

Already I'm screwing up, and it rankles. I am not enjoying this practice, not even to cherish the sensation of having twenty minutes a day to not pray/not listen/not think. I can't seem to focus my mind, and it's driving me bonkers.

One day early in June I sit in our living room to undertake my Centering Prayer practice. I've already set the kitchen timer for twenty minutes, so I'm ready to roll. I sit down on the ottoman, which is backless and therefore not very comfortable. I figure I get at least two holy brownie points for that. The phrase I've chosen for my sacred non-mantra is "peace, be still."

The first thing I notice is the sudden noise around me. It's lunchtime during the first Wednesday of the month, and I'd forgotten that it's siren day. At noon on that day, the city of Cincinnati always tests its emergency siren system. Waaaaaaaaaaaaaaail. *I wonder what would happen in a real emergency,* speculates Monkey Mind. *What kind of situation would they use this siren to tell us about? Just a tornado, or a terrorist attack? Oh crikey, what would I do in a terrorist attack?*

"Peace, be still," whispers Spiritual Mind. I let it go. I picture that thought floating away on a sailboat, stark against a bright blue sky. I hear a dog bark. A toddler fusses on the sidewalk outside.

You know, it would be quieter in this room if we replaced those eighty-five-year-old windows with double panes, suggests Monkey Mind. That's a really good idea! I have been meaning to research that possibility. How much would it cost, though? Would we be able to afford it while also paying for Jerusha's new school for next year? Could we match the old six-over-one window panes, or do they not make that style anymore?

"Peace, be still," says Spiritual Mind, a little more firmly this time.

I sigh and try to listen for God. *Or maybe that was God,* interjects Monkey Mind. *Maybe God is telling you to replace the windows and do your bit for the environment. Newer windows are so much more energy efficient. God cares about creation, you know!*

"Peace. Be. Still."

We start again. Peace is such a beautiful thought. *Peace, be still,* hums Monkey Mind. *What are the lyrics to that hymn?* "The winds and the waves shall obey Thy will, Peace, be still! Whether the wrath of the storm tossed sea, Or demons or men, or whatever it be. . . ." *Hey, did the guy who wrote that hymn really think that demons were attacking him? That is so bizarre. What would that feel like, if demons were real and they just went around attacking people? What if a demon tried to possess me like in that movie where—*

"Shut the hell up!" yells Spiritual Mind.

I'm starting to understand what the phrase "spiritual warfare" is all about. As the days wear on, "Peace, be still," verges on a spiteful joke. I am not getting this. I begin coming up with every kind of excuse to avoid the practice. During my lunch break when I've planned to hunker down and just do it, I realize that Onyx has not yet been walked today. I'm sure he desperately needs to get some fresh air and check his pee-mail from other dogs in the neighborhood. Shouldn't I take care of that first? And when we return from that, there are only forty minutes left in my lunch hour. If I spend twenty of those minutes doing Centering Prayer, I'll only have twenty minutes left to make and eat my lunch. Hmmm. Don't those mindfulness teachers also say that you should never eat in a rush?

I am simply not getting along with Centering Prayer. What surprises me about my abject failure is that it's not because I'm uncomfortable with silence. I'm a veteran of a number of silent retreats; I love being free of small talk, able to dream my own dreams. What little religious upbringing I had as a kid happened when my mom started taking us to Quaker Meeting when I was nine years old. (I think she figured that it was dangerous to grow up with absolutely no exposure to religion.

If we didn't have organized religion as children, what would we rebel against later?) Although silence at Meeting was as hard for me as it would be for any garrulous fifth grader, I secretly looked forward to the long hour of tranquility interrupted occasionally by the sound of the growling stomachs of those who'd unwisely skipped breakfast. And as an adult, since I'm an editor and writer, some amount of silence is a necessary—and pleasurable—part of my work.

So if it's not the expectation of silence that's the problem for me, what's the trouble here? I think it's the expectation that I'll actually (not) pray, (not) listen, and (not) think during this time. As Bourgeault puts it, there is silence and then there is *silence*. It's great to take a walk in the woods, but if your head is swimming with activity and worries then the silence is only external. She distinguishes between free silence, like the lovely hall-pass silence I find on retreat, and intentional silence, which is about training the promiscuous, free-floating mind and "almost always feels like work." (You think?) The problem, as the Buddhists have long identified, is that when our monkey mind jumps from tree limb to tree limb, it brings the rest of the monkey along for the ride.

Each day I conclude that Centering Prayer can wait until later . . . except that "later" doesn't exactly arrive anytime that day, or the next.

*Even if you did nothing in your meditation but bring your heart
back, and place it again in our Lord's presence, though it went
away again every time you brought it back,
your hour would be very well employed.*
—FRANCIS DE SALES

Before I know it, I haven't attempted to sit down for Centering Prayer in five days.

"The only thing wrong you can do in this prayer is to get up and walk out," wrote Father Keating. I think he meant this to be helpful advice—*hey, kids, you're a success so long as you don't give up!* It's like how nowadays at children's events they get a trophy for just showing up at YMCA soccer or participating on a team. My daughter even got a "roller skating party" badge for her Girl Scout vest. In my day we'd have had to lash a tent together with dental floss if we wanted a badge.

But I would have been very proud of my tent. I don't think that all the grace-filled badges and trophies that kids receive nowadays mean much to them, since they are keenly aware that they didn't do anything to deserve it. So it is with me and Centering Prayer—Keating and Bourgeault can *tell* me again and again that I'm good enough and smart enough, but I'm the one inhabiting this particular monkey mind, and I'm the one who knows that I can't cut it.

And so I quit. Just like that. Although I've failed to varying degrees at the five spiritual practices I've tried so far this year, I've never stopped cold turkey before. I am exhausted by the artificiality of trying to pray this way. I despise its formality and coldness.

I also despise myself, because contemplative prayer is about to join a long list of prayer methods I've already tried and failed. There were the slim, discreetly flowered prayer journals I kept in my purse in high school and part of college, when as a relatively new Christian I recorded my prayers for my own and other people's problems. Mostly my own. Then there was the down-on-my-knees phase, when I attempted to pray every morning and evening in what I thought must be the holiest posture ever devised—holy because it was so uncomfortable that it was difficult to think about anything besides my sore knees.

These were followed years later by the prayer-walking phase, when I would strap baby Jerusha into a stroller and try to incorporate prayer into my daily walks. However, I kept getting distracted by the weather, thoughts about work, anxieties about child rearing, and willing myself to remember that tomorrow was trash day. This was followed by a much longer phase where I prayed haphazardly and without much forethought—which is where I still am most days. Apart from reciting the Lord's Prayer with Jerusha at bedtime, my prayers are ad hoc and freeform, arising out of necessity for the people I love. The only thing I can be proud of in my prayer life is that when I promise to pray for someone, I actually do it.

Insights from two other people help me let go of Centering Prayer and stop beating myself up. First, I consult a writer acquaintance, Claudia, about my failures. She's a prayer warrior and the author of a terrific book on Saint Teresa of Avila (not to be confused with Thérèse of Lisieux, who, as I mentioned in the opening chapter, was a first-class diva). When I confess to Claudia my complete inadequacies in Centering Prayer, she asks a simple question: why am I doing this?

That's a very good question. The short answer, of course, is "for the book about reading and practicing spiritual classics," but that doesn't explain why I agreed to the whole memoir experiment in the first place. The real reason is that underneath all my cynicism, I felt hungry for God. I had hoped that Centering Prayer would be like getting my car battery jump-started on an icy day, and everything would suddenly roar back into life. But my spiritual battery remains incommunicado.

So Claudia lays this lovely paraphrase on me from St. Teresa:

> Place yourself in the presence of Christ.
> Don't wear yourself out thinking.
> Simply speak with your Beloved.
> Delight in him.
> Lay your needs at his feet.
> Acknowledge that he doesn't have to allow you in his presence.

(But he does!)
There is a time for thinking,
And a time for being.
Be.
With him.

Teresa, one of the great mystics of the Christian church, has given me a gold star just for trying! Claudia has made my day.

I also get a nod of comfort from my colleague Vinita, who is something of an expert in the spiritual disciplines and actually leads retreats on *lectio divina*, which I sheepishly confess to having already flunked a couple of months ago. "And now I'm a Centering Prayer dropout," I admit.

She cocks an eyebrow and considers me for a moment across the breakfast table before weighing in with her raspy alto voice. I've always loved Vinita's speaking voice, which has an unexpected Southern slowness for someone who actually grew up in Kansas. I hope she's not about to use it to bust my chops.

"You know, in other world religions, this kind of deep prayer and meditation is not something a person would undertake without a teacher," she says. I exhale. She is offering me a face-saving theological out. "That's true in Sufism, Hasidic Judaism, and other traditions. And for Christian Centering Prayer, Keating would teach the method and reasons for it at retreats, to groups. It's just not the kind of practice anyone should try alone," she concludes.

So I say good-bye to Centering Prayer. Maybe we'll be friends later in life, when I've grown up enough to calm my mind and the practice makes me less agitated rather than more. But I'm not holding my breath, either figuratively or literally.

THE JESUS PRAYER

A few years ago I interviewed an Orthodox Christian bookseller for an article I was writing, and we wound up having a wonderful conversation in which we discovered a shared love for several different authors. He said that I might like a book called *The Philokalia*, which I'd never heard of before. "That's a book that's gonna kick your ass," he promised. It struck me as a sterling recommendation.

Now, casting about for a replacement prayer practice, I pick up *The Philokalia*—which at first glance seems to be a kind of greatest hits of the top monks of Orthodox Christianity. I want to learn what they have to say about the Jesus Prayer, one of the most simple and elegant prayers I've ever seen: "Lord Jesus Christ, Son of God, have mercy on me, a sinner."

That's it, the whole enchilada. Four wee clauses packed with gospel truths: Christ's lordship, his relationship to God, our need for forgiveness, our propensity to sin. It's a prayer that Christians have been saying since about the fourth century. It's a prayer I might even have a chance of living out.

But right away *The Philokalia* starts kicking my ass in a wholly different way than the bookseller probably intended. The Jesus Prayer is everywhere and nowhere in its four hundred pages, which are typeset in a font so small I think that there must be no Orthodox Christians over the age of forty-five. The book is a rummage sale of spiritual instruction: we've got aphorisms, we've got stories, we've got advice for future monks. I try to skip ahead to some of the texts on prayer—I've only got two weeks left in June now that I've screwed up Centering Prayer, so time is of the essence—but it's not all that obvious where these texts are located. The ones with *prayer* in the title are way over my head since I've been to precisely one Orthodox service in my life, and my chief memory is that I spent it wondering if we would ever sit down. (We didn't. There weren't even chairs at the church.)

I should have suspected that people who can stand up for hours in their religious services are tougher than I am. So maybe I shouldn't be surprised that when I do find the lowdown about the Jesus Prayer in a section called "Directions to Hesychasts," it sounds more complicated than merely repeating twelve magic words over and over. (*Hesychast*, by the way, is not a dread disease, which is what it sounds like, but someone engaged in a form of mystical prayer. So now you know.) The Fathers actually break down the Jesus Prayer phrase by phrase and tell monks what they're supposed to be learning and thinking at each stage. Not surprisingly, "Lord Jesus Christ, Son of God," is designed

Let the Jesus prayer cleave to your breath—and in a few days you will see it in practice.
—Hesychius, quoted in "Directions to Hesychasts" 22,
   The Philokalia

to lead us back to Jesus Christ himself. Check. "Have mercy on me" turns the tables and invites self-scrutiny, "since he [the praying sinner] cannot as yet pray about himself." Okay, struggling with prayer does sound like me. Check. But then the praying person is supposed to jump into spiritual hyperdrive by gaining "the experience of perfect love."

Hang on. By word twelve I'm supposed to experience *perfect love*? It seems a lot to ask.

So while on the surface I'm not fighting with the Jesus Prayer to the same degree I battled with Centering Prayer, apparently it's not enough to say it fifty times a day in my head, which is the modest goal I've set for myself. I sprinkle these recitations throughout the day rather than squeeze them in to a single session, and I like the feeling of remembering the Prayer when I am grateful, frustrated, or catch myself judging someone else. I honestly think it is helping me to remember Christ's love throughout the day. I especially love a suggestion I read in a secondary source: that when we recite the first part of the prayer, we should inhale ("Lord Jesus Christ, Son of God"), and then exhale through the rest ("have mercy on me, a sinner"). The idea is that we inhale divinity and then exhale our own sin. I enjoy imagining myself as a tree in reverse: taking in the good stuff and blowing out the bad.

But am I feeling perfect love? Not so much.

As I read on in *The Philokalia* I discover that some of the monks get a little anxious about letting neophytes sit in the driver's seat of the Jesus Prayer without a bona fide license. They think these twelve words are so spiritually powerful that demons (who seem always at the ready in Orthodox Christianity) will take advantage of newbies who aren't keeping their gaze fixed on Christ. Callistus says, for example, that the devil may try to trick me by "coloring the air to resemble light" or "producing flame-like forms." However, it seems to me that such trippy manifestations of demonic activity would be a pretty obvious clue that something's awry, so I choose to ignore him.

It also sounds like these cautions are intended for monks who feel themselves superior and imagine they've achieved a certain level of holiness. They've left humility behind. Not me, though. Not for nothing have I failed for six months continuously! If demons only attack those who think they're experts at spirituality, then one of the benefits of finding out you pretty much suck is that it's like spraying a demonic version of Off. When my assigned demons see that I'm hardly about to get cocky about the Jesus Prayer, they'll yawn and wander off to play poker.

AT THE EMPATHY-FREE DENTIST

It's during this time that I head off to the dentist chair for some minor work. I secretly call my practitioner the Asperger's dentist, because he's a fascinating example of someone who can be very good at his job—and talk endlessly about it whether you are interested or not—but be unburdened by human facilities such as understanding. He is almost wholly empathy-free.

I first cottoned on to that fact shortly after I'd had my miscarriage. I had canceled, and then rescheduled, some dental work for which I needed conscious sedation. He asked me why I had come back after canceling, and I responded that I'd had a miscarriage and was no longer pregnant, so I could have the anesthesia after all. I was admirably matter-of-fact when I laid this out, but in truth I was struggling not to cry.

Most men, upon hearing about a woman's pregnancy loss, react in one of two ways. The sensitive ones will utter some version of "I'm sorry," and you can see in their eyes that they truly are. The others become visibly uneasy and do their best to change the subject immediately or flee the room. Dr. Asperger had a completely different reaction: he started to laugh. He then launched into what he promised was a funny story about a woman who had had a miscarriage right there in his office.

Gesturing across the hall, where the allegedly hilarious incident had taken place, he announced that a patient had started bleeding out one day in the examining chair. "She was just, like, crying and stuff!" he said. "That lady was a mess! We had to call her doctor right then and there."

He laughed some more as I tried to figure out what, exactly, he found so amusing. The dental assistant, obviously horrified by his lack of sensitivity, gestured madly to cue him to lay off.

Yes, gentle reader, I hear your cry. Why didn't I just get up right then and walk out? This man was not created to deal with human patients.

But he's the only Cincinnati dentist in my insurance network who will knock me out cold for relatively minor procedures, which is a quality I value in a dentist. I'm stuck with him.

Things have improved since then, as I've adjusted to Dr. Asperger's quirky ways and his tendency to take up ten minutes of a fifteen-minute appointment telling me about his board exams, the embryology of the human tooth, or his latest plans for renovating the office. The truth is that despite the complete absence of a bedside manner, he does excellent work.

Which is why I'm here today. Since I don't need full sedation this time, I'm getting numb. "How you doing with the nitrous?" the assistant Trish asks solicitously, a little too loudly, as one might ask a nursing home patient how he is enjoying his lime Jell-O.

"It's fantashtic, acshually," I slur.

"Great!" she beams. "I'm so glad you're enjoying it!" She is delighted to see me getting high. And for a while, this is how it goes in the dentist's chair: I am loose and listening to my iPod, the dentist drills and does his thing, and my mind rambles off. Until . . . crap! That *hurts*! Something has gone wrong, and I am reduced to a quivering jellyfish, trying hard to be brave but desperately wanting it to be over. They numb me up again and wait a few more minutes.

"How's that feel now, hon? Do you feel numb?" Trish asks, all concern. I am well enough to note the oxymoronic nature of this statement—if I'm numb, isn't the point *not* to feel anything?—but not well enough to comment. I just open up my jaw and bear it. It's like a nightmare.

And so I pray.

This, at last, is when I experience deeper success with the Jesus Prayer. I need so desperately to get out of my own head that I just sit there, listening to Enya and saying *lordjesuschristsonofGodhave-mercyonmeasinner* over and over again in my mind. It's surprisingly

calming and helpful. *Lordjesuschristsonof Godhavemercyonmeasinner. Lordjesuschristsonof Godhavemercyonmeasinner.*

*"Prayer of the heart" occurs when the Prayer moves from
merely mental repetition, forced along by your own effort, to
an effortless and spontaneous self-repetition of the Prayer that
emanates from the core of your being, your heart.*
—FREDERICA MATHEWES·GREEN

A surprising thought occurs to me as I sit in that chair begging
for Christ's mercy: I've never actually forgiven Dr. Asperger for his
social lapse after my miscarriage. I already know in my heart that he
didn't intend to be cruel, so why am I hanging on to this old injury?
Whether he made the comment out of his own discomfort or out of
complete ignorance about human psychology doesn't matter. He was
not trying to hurt me.

By reminding me I'm a sinner, the Jesus Prayer has allowed this
scar to rise up gently before my consciousness, showing me that I'm
hardly fit to judge my dentist when I am unkind to others, usually
unintentionally but occasionally intentionally, all the time. The Jesus
Prayer reminds me who I am in Christ—and just as important, who
I'm not. I'm not God, with authority to judge others. I am a sinner,
just like my dentist.

And so I forgive him, right then while he's drilling, drilling, drilling.
I forgive you, Doctor, and I hope you feel God's love today.
Lordjesuschristsonof Godhavemercyonmeasinner.

unorthodox sabbath

What we are depends on what the Sabbath is to us.
—ABRAHAM JOSHUA HESCHEL

7:15 AM. The alarm goes off, and I'm immediately presented with my first opportunity to break the laws of the Orthodox Jewish Sabbath I'm observing this month. Despite a fog of disorientation, I recognize the dilemma right away: I have an electric alarm clock. I should have shrouded it in a cloth so I wouldn't be tempted to so much as look at it. Instead, I've forgotten to deprogram it, and the digital hussy beeps at me with growing insistence. I decide that it would be more *shalom*-inducing for everyone in the family if I turn the alarm off, so there it is: my first violation of the Orthodox Jewish Sabbath. I've been awake for approximately fifteen seconds.

The second transgression comes moments later at the front door. Each morning, Onyx follows me downstairs with more enthusiasm than we see from him the entire rest of the day, bounding and leaping in anticipation of his first outing. It isn't actually much of an outing—I open the front door and let him pee in the neighbor's yard. (To be fair, the dogs have an unspoken reciprocal arrangement whereby Bailey, the neighbor's dog, pees almost exclusively in *our* yard, so this isn't as rude as it sounds.) Only today, I stand frozen at the front door with my hand halfway to the knob. The alarm system. Phil programmed it last night after I went to bed, as is his faithful habit, and neither of us thought to alter the usual pattern.

If it weren't for Onyx, I'd just wait another hour until everyone else is up; I'm in no hurry to go outside. But the wretch is prancing from paw to paw in his obvious need to use the facilities. He even woofs at me, a low, guttural single bark that is as rare as it is pointed. Isn't there some law that on the Sabbath, it's permissible to rescue an ox who falls into a ditch, rather than making the animal suffer a whole day before liberation? Right! There is a clear scriptural precedent for animals in need. I key in the password and open the door, Onyx springing immediately out of sight. And then, unthinkingly and out of pure habit, I switch off the porch light to welcome the day before remembering that I'm not supposed to flip light switches, which violates the injunction, "Do not kindle a fire." Strike three.

My Sabbath experiment has been underway for approximately three and a half minutes, and already I am worthy of stoning.

AN ARCHITECTURE IN TIME

My project this month is to attempt a viable practice of an Orthodox Jewish Sabbath, complete with no driving, no use of electricity, no cooking, and of course none of my usual work. My companion on this journey is Abraham Joshua Heschel (1907–1972), who wrote an enduring 1951 classic called *The Sabbath* that is still in print. I figure that Heschel's an expert on the Sabbath. Born into a dynastic Hasidic family in Poland, the scion of generations of famous rebbes, he fled the Nazis in the late 1930s by coming to England and then America. He spent many years as a professor at Jewish Theological Seminary in New York, helping to raise up a whole generation of American rabbis. He remained observant of Jewish laws and rituals, true to his faith and his impressive heritage, and did a great deal to encourage American Jews to revive or strengthen ancient practices that some had abandoned as antiquated.

His book *The Sabbath* was not a how-to guide for creating a restful Sabbath in the unlikely environment of busy, prosperous postwar America. It didn't draw on the self-help psychology that was then becoming popular to tell Jews that if they would only observe God's weekly cease-and-desist order, they would experience inner peace or stronger families. Rabbi Heschel leaves such low-hanging fruit for others and goes after a more intriguing argument: *how* does the Sabbath carve out holiness?

Most of life, he says, is a struggle to conquer the space around us: we conquer space when we pay our mortgage, battle any kudzu that threatens to encroach in the yard, or venture forth from our homes to wage the incessant war that is earning a living. But it's a tradeoff. We can only conquer that space, he explains, when we sacrifice *time*. And after some years of this, a surprising thing

> *Blessed are You, our God, Creator of time and space, who*
> *separates the holy from the mundane.*
> —TRADITIONAL PRAYER WHEN
> ENDING THE SABBATH

happens: we come to dread blank time without that war of busyness, because here we have to face the truth of who we are and what we're doing. Many people persist in a state of perpetual dread of empty time because they live entirely in the world of space. That's a luxury that Orthodox Jews cannot afford, however, because God saddled them with the Sabbath. And they, in turn, offer to share it with everybody else. (Um, thanks!)

The Sabbath may be the Jews' great gift to the world, but Rabbi Heschel says this innovation can only be appreciated when compared to other areas where Jews have not exactly been leaders. Architecture, for instance. While other religions have been busy constructing their Domes of the Rock (Islam), Hagia Sophias (Eastern Orthodoxy), and soaring cathedrals like St. Peter's and Notre Dame (Roman Catholicism), Jews are hard-pressed to claim a single unforgettable building of worship. I reflect on a college trip to Israel and realize this observation rings true to my experience: all of the finest architecture belonged to Muslims and to Christians of too many persuasions to count, who were obviously trying to one-up each other as well as pay homage to their God. Jews don't have many synagogues that are world famous simply for how they look; the eminent ones are known because Rabbi So-and-So presided there, or the congregation's Torah scroll once unfurled itself and gobbled a Nazi. They're generally nondescript buildings with nary a hint of the vitality hidden within.

So, Jews don't have fantastic buildings. What they do have is the Sabbath, which Rabbi Heschel claims is their "palace in time." Here's how he describes it:

> He who wants to enter the holiness of the day must first lay down the profanity of clattering commerce, of being yoked to toil. He must go away from the screech of dissonant days, from the nervousness and fury of acquisitiveness and the betrayal in embezzling his own life. He must say farewell to manual work and learn to understand that the world has already been created and will survive without the help of man.

It may sound like good news that the world can jolly well survive without me, but I actually find this notion a little depressing. Much of my world—my helicopter parenting, my workaholism, my ceaseless lists—is predicated on the comforting fantasy that I am indispensible.

But as a pastor I know likes to say, graveyards are filled with indispensible people. The Sabbath reminds us that we're always pointing toward eternity—which is a heavy, and often unwelcome, truth.

LIVING THE SABBATH

It's not until I start trying to *live* the Sabbath practice that its ideological weight begins to lift. Now, I'm not entirely new to the whole Sabbath concept. In our house we have a few rules about Sundays: they are primarily for worship and rest. Everybody has to go to church unless they're sick, bleeding, out of town, or in some event that can't be rescheduled, such as the Olympics or their own death. And there are whole lists of things we do and don't do: Unless there's an emergency need for chocolate, we don't go shopping. We don't do work or homework. We often take naps, have folks over for supper, or enjoy a family movie night at home. It's an unplugged kind of day.

So by twenty-first-century American standards, we're already almost Puritan in our observance of the Sabbath. Just by trying to keep it a special day, a day when we don't work and are free to relax with friends and not accomplish much, we're pushing back against the culture. But now, we're going to step it up. We're going to be Orthodox Jews.

It all starts on the first Saturday of July, when I am running around like a Jewish grandmother trying to get everything ready. Well, not quite like a Jewish grandmother, because she would have made all these preparations on Friday in anticipation of a Saturday Sabbath. Because our lives are already engineered to slow down on Sundays, we're going to observe our Sabbath from sundown on Saturday to sundown on Sunday. It's kind of cheating, but it's our best shot at actual Sabbath compliance.

Every person must carry the holiness of Shabbat to
hallow the other days of the week.
—REBBE NACHMAN OF BRASLAV

The first step is cleaning out my office on Saturday afternoon, filing things away and shutting down the electronics. It's rare for me to turn off my computer. My husband is always riding me about this, saying that I don't need to have nine applications open at once, and that I should actually shut the whole system down at the end of a working day. I almost never do, however; I like knowing that I can pop into my office for a few minutes in the evening to check my e-mail or have a go at Facebook without booting up all over again. Phil sighs in exasperation. My Apple laptop is old, he explains to me. He has christened it the Granny Smith. It deserves a rest now and again.

For the first time in a long while, it is going to get one. I power it down and then organize all of the letters, book proposals, and books that clutter my desk into tidy piles. Then, I close the door to my office. It already feels like a victory just to declare that all of these seemingly urgent items can wait until Monday morning. In fact, I don't even have to look at them.

THE TENT OF PEACE

This office orderliness has to do with inviting the *shalom* of the Sabbath before the day even officially kicks off. Rabbi Heschel writes that for six of seven days, Jews include in their evening prayers a petition that God will "guard" their going out and coming in, which is based on a promise in Psalm 121. But on the Sabbath, the prayer is different: instead of requesting protection from harm, it declares that God will "embrace us with a tent of . . . peace." Maybe the Sabbath is similar to the way I feel on a winter's night when, clad in fleece pajamas, I finally crawl under goosedown covers and rest in the knowledge that nothing more will be demanded of me that day. God will embrace me with the tent of his peace.

At least, that's the hope. It turns out that there's a whole lot of work involved in pitching a tent of peace. For starters, I have a major dinner to conjure out of whole cloth. I buy the challah bread at a marvelous local bakery owned by Mormons—because if anyone knows how to bake a great challah, it would be a Mormon, right? For the other dishes, I'm on my own. As I was reminded when attempting kitchen mindfulness back in March, I enjoy cooking, but preparing for the Sabbath is more challenging than it appears.

The Sabbath meal is supposed to be over-the-top special, signaling by every available means that the Sabbath is the most holy day of the week, insinuating itself into every nook and cranny of life. I like the idea of this, but it's troublesome to put in practice. At the last minute, I'm trying to download instructions about the prayers for the meal, chop the strawberries for a fruit salad, and convince my daughter that yes, it really is time to turn off the television. I also have to turn the lights on upstairs and set the DVR for *Masterpiece: Mystery.* There's a lot to remember. It's unclear why Rabbi Heschel's book lacks a check-list.

The clock ticks furiously in my head as we count down to the candle lighting. I've got to hurry because after the candles are lit, the Sabbath will officially begin, and you can't sneak any activities like putting flowers in water or turning off the oven. It's almost like everything goes into Sabbath freeze-frame for approximately twenty-five hours. (And yes, that's twenty-five hours, not twenty-four. To be on the safe side, rabbis established the rules for the Sabbath so we have to refrain from working before the sun begins to set on Sabbath eve until after it has completely set on the Sabbath Day, just so we don't do something truly evil, like use scissors to snip a coupon while there's still a streak of pink in the sky.)

The first thing our family does is light the candles, a ritual that is supposed to happen eighteen minutes before the Sabbath. I'm the star here, as the lighting is always done in a prescribed way by the mother of the house. She lights them, then waves her hands around the flames in a gesture of bringing the Sabbath peace into the heart of the family. I'm not quite certain of this movement, having only a vague recollection of Tevye's wife in *Fiddler on the Roof.* So instead of drawing the Sabbath toward us, I symbolically blow it out: my over-vigorous waving has snuffed a candle and I have to relight. I've already improvised somewhat with the candles, just using the ones we have on hand and not worrying about any nagging rules about the height of the candles or how many there should actually be. We haven't even started the Sabbath yet, and already I have performance anxiety.

Then we commence with the prayers. The Sabbath prayers aren't long, but they involve a surprising amount of physical action. We all traipse over to the kitchen sink to wash our hands—right over left—and recite a special prayer. Back at the table, there is a prayer for the Mormon-baked challah, and one for the grape juice we're using as a cheat for sweet kosher wine. I show off by reciting these in Hebrew, one of the few things I remember from the semester I spent teaching fourth and fifth graders prayerbook Hebrew at a Reconstructionist synagogue that was so liberal it didn't bat an eye at hiring a Gentile fresh out of Protestant seminary. I'm glad I still remember these prayers by heart, because there's comfort in reciting them in the language that has been used for millennia around the world.

My favorite part of our short Sabbath ritual is the blessings. Traditionally, these are done by the man of the house, who blesses his wife and children. Phil gamely lays his hands on my head and tries not to crack up as he calls me a "woman of excellence," drawing from the Bible's prescription for the ideal woman in Proverbs 31. That passage has always bothered me in its sexism (I'm going to be judged on whether I can weave purple cloth?), but there's something wholly different about hearing it recited by candlelight by someone who actually loves me, even if he is struggling not to laugh as he says, "Many women have done excellently, but you surpass them all."

Then we both lay hands on Jerusha's head and give her a parental blessing. The traditional blessing for a daughter petitions God to make her like Sarah, Rebecca, Rachel, and Leah, which is not exactly the blessing I'd wish on my girl: *May you be a micromanager, a liar, a whiner, and a cheat!* On the other hand, it's a reminder that all of us frail, flawed, clawing people have a place in the distinctly wooly kingdom of God, so despite my half-year of failing at various spiritual practices, maybe there is hope for me yet if the Bible's standards for women are so low. At least, this is what I am thinking about as I gently rest my hands on Jerusha's head. She apparently is thinking about dinner, which is getting colder by the minute as we improvise our way through these candle lightings, washings, and prayers. Jerusha sighs dramatically and wonders aloud if we are *ever* going to eat already.

The dinner of roast chicken, carrots, and potatoes is delicious and unhurried. Afterward, we carry the dishes to the sink, though I'm not at all sure that's kosher. There are specific rules about not carrying things on the Sabbath. But I'm too OCD to bear the thought of leaving them out overnight, so I use Onyx as my excuse. It would be cruel to tempt a good dog beyond what he can bear by leaving highly lickable dishes on a table he can reach without difficulty.

We spend the evening in quiet pursuits. So far, so good.

THE THIRTY-NINE PROHIBITIONS

The Jewish Sabbath comes with an impressive list of things to avoid—thirty-nine categories of things, to be exact. In advance of my Sabbath experiment, I've glanced over the categories and identified a few that I shouldn't have to worry about. I'm not likely to flay something anytime soon, so I'm in good shape on that score. I also don't regularly tan animal hides on a Sunday. Whew!

I can't work, of course. But it's not just work that we're called to resist on the Sabbath—it's any creative activity. However things are when the Sabbath begins are how they need to remain until the Sabbath ends—no washing, cutting, cleaning, painting, or the like. I'm not supposed to change anything from its original state. Even if I were allowed to light a fire or flick on the electric range, I can't boil anything (which could cause a chemical change), bake anything, or even toast my bread. Doing any of those things makes me a creator of sorts, and that role is *verboten* on the Sabbath. This is all designed to honor God's own example: he worked and created for six days but then took a calculated breather.

In the end, it's actually the creative restrictions that are the most difficult for me to abide. There's something so marvelously liberating about stepping back from work, especially housework, that I actually feel *more* creative, more eager to put words to paper. But I can't even

In the silence of our Sabbath observation our minds can rest, and that often leads to the freedom to learn anew how best to use our minds for the glory of God.
—MARVA DAWN

take real-time notes about my Sabbath experiment because I'm not allowed to write, turn on a computer, or vocalize cryptic reminders into the Dragon Dictation app on my iPhone. The rabbis are clear about writing: you can make one letter, and no more.

Church is another problem. I can't drive myself there, but it's several miles away so it would be a bit of a hike. I'm not keen on showing up on a sweltering July morning all sweaty, but I feel guilty about not doing my bit for the planet. Then I discover a wondrous fact: Orthodox Jews are actually supposed to count their steps on the Sabbath. That's why they try to live so close to their shul, so it's a short walk and they don't have to use a car at all. (Apparently Jews in Israel can also use a special Segway-ish vehicle called the Shabbat scooter. That sounds way cooler than my basic plan of bumming rides from my friends. So, next year in Jerusalem.)

I try to share the load among various girlfriends and my husband, so that no one gets stuck ferrying me to and from church every single week. One Sunday, I remember just before pickup time that I haven't confirmed with my friend Alethea that she's supposed to give me a ride. We hatched this plan on Wednesday, but haven't discussed it since then, and I can't exactly whip out my cell phone and give her a call. Will she remember? She does. What a *mensch*.

SHABBOS GOYIM

Alethea is just one of many people pressed into service to help me carry out my Sabbath plans. But at least I don't have to ask her to shred my toilet paper for me. That's my daughter's job.

During my first week of Sabbath observance, I actually didn't realize that I was supposed to pre-shred my own toilet paper before the Sabbath began. In my relaxing afternoon reading time that first Sunday, I learned that TP breakage violates the Sabbath law against tearing, so you're supposed to pre-shred all your TP the day before. Who knew? I gave myself a bye that first week, because surely God wouldn't strike me down for not knowing the rules. But the second week, I pre-ripped that Charmin with a vengeance, grossly overestimating how much I'd use in a twenty-five-hour period. We had leftover pre-shredded TP for two more days.

But on the third week I err on the side of being too conservative. Oops. (Note to you, dear reader: err on the *other* side. Shred half the roll; you can always use it later.) I have to call my daughter into the bathroom to shred some more TP for me, an oversight she does not let me live down for days.

Jerusha is handy in a pinch. I call her my Sabbath goy—a non-Jewish person who can perform certain services for Jews on Shabbat, like turning on the lights at the shul or babysitting the kids. I think all Jews need to keep at least one non-Jewish child in the home for this very reason. When the Sabbath comes around, it's helpful to have someone answer the phone for you, flip you a kosher burger, or tell you what's on *Headline News*. The problem, unfortunately, is that this arrangement is expressly forbidden in the Ten Commandments. Here's what Exodus 20:9–10 says about work:

> Six days you shall labor and do all your work. But the seventh day
> is a sabbath to the Lord your God; you shall not do any work—you,
> *your son or your daughter,* your male or female slave, your livestock,
> or the alien resident in your towns.

See how clever God is? He thinks ahead, and he knows that people will always oppress other people when given half a chance. Apparently I don't get to oppress Jerusha on the Sabbath, nor can I ask the goy-next-door if I can soak up her air conditioning for a while.

There are too many things to remember, and the learning curve feels steep. Part of the problem with the Jew-it-yourself approach is that I have only books to guide me. By the third week I know that if I had the whole thing to do over again, I'd enlist a small group of people to do this experiment together, take turns with some of the prep, and maybe ply each other with *kugel*. I'd also get a real-life rabbi as an advisor. Rabbi Heschel's book is beautiful, but there's an unwanted austerity in trying to keep the Sabbath without a teacher. It's not as isolating as the Ramadan fast I did in February, but it's lonely. Real Jews, at least the ones I imagine to have clustered in Rabbi Heschel's apartment in New York, linger at the dinner table singing Sabbath *zemirot* (songs) or engaging in animated debates about the Torah.

ON CHOLENT

As I live through the month of Sabbaths, I have a bone to pick with Rabbi Heschel. I find his book *The Sabbath* beautiful, but . . . nowhere does Rabbi Heschel write about practical things. Like, say, eating. Food is a huge part of a lovely Shabbos celebration, but the book takes it for granted that such feasts are effortlessly prepared by unseen kosher elves. Rabbi Heschel states, on the one hand, that it is forbidden to work on the Sabbath, but another book I'm reading claims that it's a *mitzvah* (good deed) to have a hot meal on the Sabbath. What gives? So either:

1) Cooking is not work (which it is, according to the aforementioned thirty-nine things), or

2) Someone else is shopping, planning, chopping, stirring, baking, and cleaning up afterward. Now, I'm no rocket scientist, but I'd be willing to wager that this someone's name is Mrs. Heschel.

The Orthodox Jewish Sabbath puts a lot of pressure on women: when the Sabbath begins, the house is supposed to be as spotless as it would be if you were hosting a wedding, because the Sabbath is regarded as a bride. You don't just use the everyday dishes when you're having a wedding in your home. You trot out the nicest china, the folded napkins, the fresh flowers, the candles, and Bubbe's *kaddish* cup. And you knock yourself out cooking beforehand, because the food is supposed to be magnificent.

Producing a memorable Sabbath meal isn't much of a problem on the first night, when a model Jewish mother can whip up a gorgeous spread before the sun goes down. But I'll bet even she can't summon a full hot meal with all the trimmings at lunch the next day. I determine that Sunday's Sabbath lunch will be simplicity itself: fruit, sandwiches, juice boxes. But even here I run into problems. I'm not allowed to poke a hole through my juice box, cut Jerusha's apple into wedges, or tear off a square of paper towel to clean up a spill.

A culinary breakthrough occurs when I decide to supplement Rabbi Heschel's pie-in-the-sky etherealism with a realistic helping of Jewish cookbooks. The half dozen I check out from the library prove to be a gold mine of how-to information about holidays and Sabbath meals. It is here that I first learn about *cholent.*

Cholent was invented because I'm apparently not the first person to notice a discrepancy between the ideal that you should have a hot meal on the Sabbath and the reality that all the means of producing said meal are off-limits to you. It's the main dish you would get if those authors of the *Fix It and Forget It* Crock-Pot cookbook bestsellers had been Jewish instead of Mennonite. Basically, you take a big slab of beef (no pork, please), throw it in a casserole dish with some onions, carrots, beans, potatoes, water, and barley, place it in a two-hundred-degree oven *before* you light the candles for the Sabbath, and let it roast all night long. Voila, you have a hot meal for lunch the following day. I started out highly suspicious of this recipe—what beef would be anything but shriveled after roasting for eighteen or so hours?—but it was delicious.

FEELING THE LOVE

With all of my spiritual experiments this year, I've discovered that it takes several weeks to get past the initial how-to aspects of surviving a new practice before I can delve into the spirit behind it. If there are glimpses of spiritual connection or growth (and I learned last month with Centering Prayer that there aren't always), they arise once I've settled into the practice and allow it to speak.

So it's not until the final weekend that I find myself unexpectedly longing for the spiritual peace of the Sabbath. It's been a busy, crazy week, filled with stressful deadlines at work and major decisions at home. Phil and I are feeling intense financial pressure as we write the largest nonmortgage check of our lives: a year's tuition to a private school for Jerusha. By the time Saturday afternoon rolls around, I am desperate for a break from all of these worldly anxieties, for a "palace in time."

I find peace in unexpected places: in the aroma of *cholent* wafting through the house, in the comfort of a long nap. And for me, the *shalom* also comes from rich study. The greatest gift of the Sabbath is having time set aside specifically to read. I dig out books about the Sabbath itself, and other books about Jewish life. One of these is *The Book of Lights* by novelist Chaim Potok, which has been sitting on my shelf for years alongside more oft-perused favorites like *My Name Is Asher Lev* and *The Chosen*. I'm so glad to finally mine its beauty that I go on a Chaim Potok kick for the whole month of July, reading and rereading the stories he set in the world of the ultra-Orthodox.

It's lovely to have an excuse to read fiction. Since I'm an editor and a writer, I have to be careful that what I'm reading doesn't subtly spill over into work. I don't want the reading to become a "task," and what's special about it is that I get to approach each Sunday afternoon without an agenda—something that never happens in my life. I simply pull down from the shelf whatever looks interesting at the moment.

This is in keeping with something I read in Marva Dawn's book about the Sabbath. I'd like to underline the passage but can't since I'm reading it on Sunday. I place a sticky note in the book before wondering whether removing a sticky note from its pad of yellow friends constitutes the forbidden activities of ripping and tearing. Well, it's done now. Whatever.

Marva Dawn's a Christian who draws on Jewish traditions. She looks to the Sabbath as a way off the treadmill of evaluating our worthiness based on how many items we've crossed off a list each day.

I am usually guilty of measuring my worth by my productivity: did I meet my word quota today? The Sabbath, to paraphrase Dawn, is God's way of letting us know that he's not following us around with a clipboard, quantifying his love based on how much we've done for him lately. He's our parent, and "parents raise children primarily by who they *are*, not by what they *do*."

This unconditional acceptance is in direct contrast to everything the Israelites had experienced in Egypt. According to Old Testament

The Sabbath is the most radical commandment because it's a decision not to let your life be defined by Pharaoh's production-consumption rat race.

scholar Walter Brueggemann, another person I'm reading this month, the fourth commandment is primarily about stopping work. In the Egyptian system, no Israelite *ever* got to stop making bricks, and Pharaoh would tighten the screws if there wasn't a constant uptick in 24/7 production. Brueggemann thinks that Pharaoh's system is a great producer of anxiety; there will always be more bricks to make, and no one can ever stop. But the Sabbath teaches us that we're not slaves, even to ourselves.

I don't want to be part of Pharaoh's system. So when Jerusha interrupts my reading one Sabbath afternoon and asks me to play a game with her, I say yes. My reading isn't as important as simply playing with her, which I don't do enough of on non-Sabbath days. As we get out the Dogopoly board and pieces, I have a momentary twinge about the kosherness of playing this particular game on the Sabbath when it's all about capitalism and becoming the canine version of Donald Trump. It's *treyf* (unkosher) to handle money on the Sabbath. But do the rules relax if the money is pastel pink, yellow, and blue?

I realize I don't actually care. The Gospel of Mark claims that the Sabbath was made for me, not the other way around, and I'm going to play Dogopoly today. Jerusha and I play for nearly four hours, which has to be a record for the longest single stretch of game play I've had since childhood without having to do something else, like fold laundry or cook a meal. She trounces me, building her empire on the Great Dane and the Saint Bernard, the Dogopoly equivalents of Boardwalk and Park Place, as we share an afternoon of laughter. It is a good Sabbath.

thanksgiving every day

Give thanks in all circumstances,
for this is God's will for you in Christ Jesus.
—1 THESSALONIANS 5:18 (NIV)

"What's your spiritual practice this month?" an acquaintance asks me as we chat on the phone about other things.

I have a cheerful reply at the ready. "Gratitude. You know, just being grateful for all the little things."

"Well! That should be easy compared to fasting and that weird Sabbath thing you did last time," she observes. "Even a little kid can practice gratitude."

I hope she's right that gratitude is going to be the bunny slope of my year of spiritual experiments. In fact I'm planning on it, because I need a break after the steep learning curve of Sabbath keeping. We're on vacation for the first part of this month, and frankly, I want an easily transportable practice that won't require much extra time, planning, or hand wringing.

I'm not alone in attempting to be more grateful. These days, there's an upsurge of research on gratitude, mostly about how cultivating thankfulness can improve our lives. In keeping with the lighter, less demanding theme of this month, I've decided to bypass a single spiritual classic in favor of a number of different shorter writings on gratitude. I want to know how to become more grateful—and whether doing so will make a difference in my life. Much of what I read promises that it will. In one nine-week study, research subjects were randomly assigned to different groups, including one asked to list annoying things in their daily lives—stupid drivers, messy houses, dwindling bank accounts. Another group was asked to catalog positive things that they felt set them apart or made their lives better than other people's. The result? The folks who counted their blessings reported fewer physical complaints, better relationships, and more optimism about the future. In all, the researchers concluded, they were 25 percent happier than the people who were asked to focus on daily hassles.

There are even links between gratitude and sleep. Researchers at the University of Manchester in England have found that people who filled out "gratitude questionnaires" just before falling asleep slept longer and deeper than study participants who didn't count their blessings just before bed. Apparently, worrywarts and ingrates can look forward to sleepless nights and infomercials for the Bowflex at three in the morning.

Who wouldn't want to sleep better, feel happier, and enjoy optimal health? Count me in.

THE GRATITUDE DIARIES

I start the month with three simple daily practices:

1) I will write down five things I'm grateful for in a little journal. (In fact, given current research on gratitude and sleep, I'm

If the only prayer you said in your whole life was "thank you,"
that would suffice.

—MEISTER ECKHART

going to do this just before I go to bed in hopes of warding off my frequent insomnia.)

2) I will write or talk to at least one friend or family member each day, detailing why I'm grateful for that person.

3) If negative thoughts plague me, I will drive them away by reviewing the gratitude journal and stepping up my efforts to focus on the positive.

My first forays into gratitude are superficial. On vacation the first week of August, we get upgraded to a fantastic two-room suite at a Chicago hotel I found for a song online. The upgrade makes that day's happy list. Also on the list is a fun mother-daughter trip to the American Girl store, where Jerusha and I meet up with an old friend and eat fancy nursery food in the tea room. The waiter even brings a special high chair so Jerusha's doll can take part in the festivities. It's a magical day, with a boat ride along the Chicago River and time to visit with other friends in the evening. The gratitude journal is a piece of cake.

The second task is more of a hurdle. I feel shy about gushing to people about how grateful I am for them. My mom, who has been laid low with pneumonia for weeks, is finally up and around. Her voice sounds more hopeful, less ravaged, on the phone. I tell her how glad I am of her recovery, and it rushes over me how lost I would be if she were to die, which of course she someday will. How can any of us ever be grateful enough for our mothers? Even the lousy ones deserve respect for bringing us into the world, and I happen to have a great one, who more than made up for the fact that my dad was such a turd. Mom sounds touched by my concern for her illness, and also by one of the birthday gifts I send her: an adorable stuffed animal version of *streptococcus pneumonia*.

The third practice, banishing negative thoughts, is where I stumble. I'm dismayed by how often negative, critical thoughts afflict me.

"You're very hard on yourself," people have told me through the years. "You're your own worst critic." That may be true—but it's also true, and unfortunate, that I'm often other people's worst critic as well. I've just gotten much better about holding my tongue, either when complaints can do nothing to help a situation or when sarcasm might hurt someone's feelings. But not to think negative thoughts in the first place? Forget about it. I cherish those nastygrams all the more because they are unexpressed, my dirty little secrets.

Does my gratitude practice reduce the frequency of negative thoughts? Not so far. Instead, it brings to the forefront my latent judgmentalism in a profoundly discomfiting way. My critical nature is one of the aspects of myself I'd most like to change. Practicing gratitude results, paradoxically, in an *increase* of negative thoughts, because some of my gratitude stems from assessing my situation as better than other people's. I'm like that Pharisee in the Gospel of Luke who opens with what seems like a statement of gratitude but devolves into a self-congratulatory declaration of superiority: "The Pharisee, standing by himself, was praying thus, 'God, I thank you that I am not like other people: thieves, rogues, adulterers, or even like this tax-collector. I fast twice a week; I give a tenth of all my income'" (18:11–12). I'd like to distance myself from this story, to tell myself that I'm not a smarmy Pharisee. But how many times this month in my gratitude practice has my thankfulness been in comparison with other people's misery? Earlier this month, when a friend's wife suddenly left him and their kids for days on end and didn't answer her cell phone, I thanked God that I have a spouse who would never pull a disappearing act. Now I make a mental note to slap myself whenever I start slipping into any prayer that opens with some version of "God, I thank you that I am not like other people."

This gratitude practice has turned out to be far from simple. It does result in greater awareness of my blessings (and it's even helped to improve my sleep), but it also functions as an artistic pentimento, bringing to the surface of my spiritual canvas many of the mistakes I've tried so diligently to paint over.

SUSTAINING GRATITUDE

Why are we so caught up with the idea of gratitude in the first place? Counting our blessings has become a Christian virtue right up there with prayer, worship, and eating green bean casserole at potlucks. Where did this come from?

Gratitude is not only the greatest of virtues, but the parent of all the others.
—CICERO

I read one study that agrees that gratitude can make us happier and healthier, but points out that it's awfully hard to sustain over time. According to this theory, human beings are naturally adaptive creatures, and one of the evolutionary mechanisms that's helped us to survive is our ability to become desensitized to anything but very recent changes. We're wired to weather just about anything because we simply acclimate ourselves to new situations. That's why we're only fleetingly affected by positive changes—a raise, a weight loss, a new romance. After a while those beneficial developments are simply absorbed into the way things are. But there's a silver lining: we can also adapt to tragic circumstances. Long-term paraplegics, for example, report the same basic levels of happiness as people with all their limbs. "When life falls apart, we'll soon get used to it—such changes in circumstance don't have to become incapacitating," the study concludes. That's the good news. "But when our lives are blessed, and things are going well, there seems something morally decrepit in how we so easily overlook how good we have it."

Yes! That's it. One of the things nagging at me this month is how I can't seem to muster up any real gratitude about being healthy. I just don't think about my good health that much, and when I write "health" in my gratitude journal, it's mostly because that's what I think I'm supposed to say. I feel guilty about this, especially because last year I had a little health scare. I went in for my first-ever mammogram and they found something. For the next month I had tests, including another (even more painful) mammogram and a needle biopsy that hurt like the devil.

At one point in the process my family doctor called me on my cell phone while I was out of town on business, telling me what the radiologist had already said: it didn't *look* like breast cancer, but I should have the biopsy procedure just to be sure, given my family's history. After I hung up the phone, I second-guessed every single thing she'd told me like a tween getting her first phone call from a boy. Did she really mean it when she said she didn't think it was cancer? What was she not telling me? And why was she calling me on my cell phone *on a Friday night?*

So when the news finally came—no cancer had been discovered—I was giddy with relief. The weather that December day was gray, cold, and rainy, but I wanted to skip and pick daisies. I felt grateful for everything in my life—my health, my crazy family, my interesting job, my warm and comfortable house. Nothing bothered me.

That feeling of overwhelming gratitude lasted approximately 2.3 days. I tried to hold on to it, but gratitude is as slippery as trout. Ingratitude happened during the Christmas season, ironically enough. Somehow, during the days of decking the halls and baking the cookies, I lost that sense of the perfection of the now. I knew I had resumed normal life when I swore like a sailor at a driver who turned directly in front of me. Yep, I was back.

CREEPING REQUIREMENTS

As my month progresses I become increasingly aware of the everyday things I take for granted, and the knowledge depresses me. I'm also conscious of a little voice in my head that follows up any expression of gratitude with a secret unexpressed desire for more. On a long flight out West to speak at a conference, I'm unexpectedly upgraded to first class (it's my lucky month for upgrades) and there enjoy an embarrassment of riches. I've already eaten lunch, but I'm given it once again, and since it might be the last hot meal ever offered to a human being on an airplane, I indulge. My seatmate is polite but engrossed in her novel, which is ideal because I hate sitting next to chatterboxes on airplanes, where there is a) no place to hide; and b) no longer any actual silverware with which to stab the loquacious smack in the larynx. With my iPhone and my noise-canceling headphones I can create my own little sanctuary with classical music while I write. I am just about perfectly content in the way of creature comforts, and as I cross the plains I try to be grateful that I'm not a member of the ill-fated Donner party who made this same trip more than a century ago. Despite some of the inconveniences of modern air travel, we've come a long way from eating each other, baby.

As much as I try to cultivate these thoughts of gratitude and intentionally return to them, here is the thought that keeps popping in my head without any effort whatsoever on my part: *I wonder if I will get upgraded on the way home.* It's humiliating how often that particular thought returns, unbidden, to spoil the moment. It's one more example of what Phil calls "creeping requirements," an engineering term for a project's tendency to become more complex all the time. Creeping requirements rob my gratitude in the moment because I'm always looking ahead to the Next Big Thing.

I'm not alone in this. If we buy the little black dress, we might have a moment of euphoria, but the purchase also necessitates the little black shoes and the silver earrings and perhaps a manicure before the cocktail party. Phil and I have noticed this all summer as our straightforward third-floor bathroom renovation has turned into a full-fledged overhaul of the second and third floors. "While we have the walls open anyway, we should update all of the wiring and bring it to code," he says. "Also, let's go ahead and insulate the attic." (What he does not mention, but which happens: "Let's be sure to insulate the attic on the hottest day of August, honey! This builds character.") The bathroom remodeling takes a backseat to the creeping requirements of while-we're-at-it syndrome. And it all sounds so prudent, so wise to want more.

The Bible talks about not coveting, and I'm intrigued that this commandment comes last of all in God's Top Ten List. Biblical lists aren't like our modern lists, where the most important thing usually comes first. Biblical lists often save the best for last: faith, hope, and LOVE, for instance. So it is with the tenth commandment, the most significant commandment of them all, because almost all of the list's other specific warnings spring from the act of coveting. We're vulnerable to committing adultery when we look longingly at someone else's attractive spouse and begin imagining life with that person; adultery begins with covetousness. We're prone to killing when the victim has something that we want. (At least, it's always this way in murder mysteries.) And even the commandments against idols and worshiping other gods stem from covetousness, from our

To be a saint is to be fueled by gratitude,
nothing more and nothing less.
—RONALD ROLHEISER

susceptibility to whatever golden calves we crave. But can gratitude save me from coveting and creeping requirements?

WHAT GRATITUDE IS NOT

Oddly, the root word for "gratitude," *gratia*, didn't start appearing in Christian literature until about eight hundred years ago. That's not to say that Christians before the High Middle Ages didn't feel gratitude—they just didn't wax on about it. In her fascinating cultural study *The Gift of Thanks*, Margaret Visser writes that although contemporary Americans and some Europeans think that gratitude is ingrained, necessary, and automatic, there are entire cultures where the concept of saying thank you is still largely absent. Some languages have no word for thanks, a fact that's hard for Americans to wrap our heads around. When European colonizers came to the New World back in the day, they were horrified that Native Americans didn't thank them for the gifts they brought—because when someone brings you smallpox as a souvenir of their homeland, the least you can do is say thank you.

In contrast, other cultures have umpteen different ways to express gratitude, based on the giver's relationship to the recipient. In Japan, if someone so much as passes you a salt shaker, you don't merely thank the giver, but instead launch into a self-abnegating apology for your existence on the planet and your annoying and perpetual need to breathe.

As I'm reading, I think about Visser's point that much of what we imagine as authentic gratitude is actually cultural expectation of what a polite, civilized person does. Politeness greases the wheels of society. We make nice. However, true gratitude rarely exists in these automatic, expected formalities. True gratitude is something else altogether.

I'm intrigued by the idea that gratitude is a relatively recent development in Western civilization. This strikes me as ironic, given how in my own experience, gratitude often springs from a remembrance of deprivation. When I get the stomach flu, I'm shocked to realize how quickly a healthy person can become a shaking mass on a chilly bathroom floor. Being sick forces us to recognize the unsung gift of health. But in twenty-first-century America, we enjoy fabulous health and longevity compared to any other time in history. So why are our bookstore shelves littered with titles on the importance of gratitude and the quest for happiness, while our pockmarked ancestors just sucked it up in silence?

Maybe we focus on gratitude because we feel guilty—and scared. We know at a deep level that we're ludicrously wealthy and healthy. We're also terrified of that ease and comfort disappearing. So we read books and articles about gratitude as a cardinal virtue not because we feel genuinely grateful, but because we're afraid of how God might smite us if we don't. There's a whole movement centered around "the power of gratitude," promising that when we say thank you for our blessings, we will "unleash unlimited abundance and happiness." You can find similar advice in books like *How to Want What You Have* and *Thank You Power* and *Focus on the Good Stuff.* The problem is that this so-called gratitude is actually more about manipulating the universe into giving us even greater blessings than it is about being grateful for the ones we already enjoy. It's like a kid after a birthday party who only sends Grandma a thank-you card because he's hoping for a more expensive present for Christmas.

I object to the proliferation of self-help books that promise that gratitude will magically make everything all better. Some years ago when the bestseller *The Secret* was all the rage, I wrote a blog review so sarcastic that I was contacted by a Dutch journalist who wanted to get the snarky American on camera to declare that merely saying thank you to the universe wasn't going to alter a person's reality. The reporter was charmed by the fact that I'd gone back through the diary of Dutch girl Anne Frank to refute the basic premise of Rhoda Byrne's self-help chartbuster: that only good things will happen to those who think good thoughts, and only bad things will happen to those who think negative thoughts. This pabulum is known as the "Law of Attraction." In the review, I pointed out how Anne Frank wasn't exactly spewing negativity with statements such as, "I don't think of all the misery but of all the beauty that remains," and, "I keep my ideals, because in spite of everything, I still believe that people are really good at heart." And yet she *was* victimized, as were millions of others. Their "attitude of gratitude" had little to do with whether they lived through the Holocaust, though some survivors have said that positive thinking helped them regroup and succeed after the war.

Gratitude didn't save Anne Frank, and it won't save us. It won't heal our diseases, make us rich, or bring us fame. We'd love to make gratitude a talisman to magically protect us from disaster, but there is nothing Christian about this; it's as pagan as the hills to stage-manage the universe into bending to our will. Gratitude is just a gentler way to force the issue, and it's a lot less messy than, say, sacrificing a bison on the altar. But using gratitude as a carrot to precipitate the universe's bestowal of a gift is as pagan as the blood sacrifice. If we ever catch ourselves thinking about how God should reward our sunny dispositions with worldly blessings, or imagining that if we're *not* grateful for what we already have that God will justifiably withhold further blessings like Santa refusing to bring toys to naughty children at Christmas, then we need to take a long and hard look at what we believe about God. God doesn't owe us anything, no matter how cheerful and uncomplaining we are. Period.

GRATITUDE FOR CHRISTIANS

It's clear to me, as I read about gratitude and try these practices myself, that gratitude is not about getting more. Or at least, it's not supposed to be. For an allegedly simple concept, gratitude is surprisingly hard to pin down; I'm much more apt to recognize what it isn't (a magical panacea, a ticket to expanded blessings) than I am able to isolate what it is. So far this month, I've been disappointed by the surface nature of most of the things in my gratitude journal. They're all so earthy, of this life: I'm grateful that my daughter's new teachers seem compassionate and caring. I'm grateful for interesting

You say grace before meals. All right. But I say grace before the concert and the opera, and grace before the play and pantomime, and grace before I open a book, and grace before sketching, painting, swimming, fencing, boxing, walking, playing, dancing and grace before I dip the pen in the ink.

—G. K. CHESTERTON

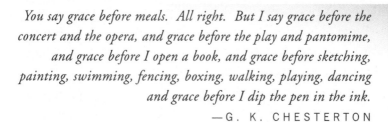

books to edit and to read. I'm inordinately grateful that peaches are in season; in fact, fresh peaches beat out health, home, family, and almost everything else on my list. Including God.

Only rarely in my journal do I hit upon spiritual topics. I'm not feeling any wells of gratitude for the things I imagine I *should* be grateful for—like, say, creation, or Jesus' sacrifice on the cross. I'm pretty much just grateful for peaches. Oh, and sweet corn, also in season. Where is God in my gratitude?

Then I stumble across something beautiful that Thomas Merton had to say about Christian gratitude:

> To be grateful is to recognize the Love of God in everything He has given us—and He has given us everything. Every breath we draw is a gift of His love, every moment of existence is a grace, for it brings with it immense graces from Him. Gratitude therefore takes nothing

for granted, is never unresponsive, is constantly awakening to new wonder and to praise of the goodness of God. For the grateful person knows that God is good, not by hearsay but by experience. And that is what makes all the difference.

Unlike the earth-bound nature of my own gratitude journal, Merton isn't focusing just on this life. Christian gratitude has got to be more expansive than the prayers I hear in my church most Sundays, as people thank God for their families, their health, their homes, their jobs, even the weather. There's nothing wrong with thanking God for those things, but if that's *all* we do, it's like claiming that the prosaic, this-worldly book of Proverbs constitutes the whole of Scripture. There is so much more to Christian experience. When the Bible commands us to be thankful, that gratitude is almost never about us or about the material comforts of our little lives. It's about being thankful *for God* and for his "steadfast love" (Ps. 118, 106, 107), not just for what he's done for us lately.

Merton suggests that every moment of existence can be a grace. I love that because, paradoxically, it takes the pressure off Christians to be so freakin' happy all the time. If every moment of existence is a grace, we can simply rest in God. It means our joy might just transcend our circumstances. Happiness in the present moment and lasting joy in God are not the same.

I recently saw a quote posted on Facebook by one M. Crane, whose aphorism claimed, "You cannot be thankful and unhappy at the same time." Within minutes, someone chimed in to say that M. Crane's maxim was a crock. I silently gave a cheer. Christians absolutely can be thankful and unhappy at the same time. In fact, we ought to be, because this world is not as God intended it. When we are in despair about a child getting leukemia, God is right there beside us feeling righteously pissed. And when we sting with the agony of betrayal,

God aches too. The gratitude that Christians feel runs deep because we're in love with a God who hates cancer even more than we do, and who knows firsthand the throb of treachery.

GRATITUDE RUN AMOK

What's surprising me about my spiritual practice this month is not that it is easy (did I mention that it isn't?), but that the simple act of counting my blessings has made gratitude start to feel more natural. Looking for the good, it turns out, often does result in finding it—even though I had not expected gratitude to also reveal unsavory aspects of my character and my superficial faith. Despite my inadequacies with this practice—my nicest stationery sits untouched in my desk drawer, as I haven't followed through with my promise to write a gushy letter of gratitude to someone new every day—I find gratitude spurting up regularly, and when it does, I act on it.

Gratitude smites me at unexpected times, most often in my travels. But it's not just the fleeting vacation euphoria of new places and people, a break from the usual routine. This well of contentment runs deeper, probably because we began the month by going on vacation to old haunts with long-loved people. There's nothing particularly new about heading to Lake Michigan with these friends we've loved for nearly two decades now, but there's a world of gratitude in these near-annual gatherings.

When Phil and I were first married, we signed up to be part of a new seminary comedy revue called Theologiggle, never expecting that four of the people we met would become some of our closest friends for life. At first, I was impressed by their humor and cleverness—we cracked ourselves up impersonating seminary professors and writing skits filled with insider jokes about Q, the elusive fifth Gospel.

But these friendships continued to flower long after graduation day. Through the years, our three families have welcomed five children and shared the joys and heartbreaks of trying to figure out how to be quality parents. And when my mom had cancer the first time, Ron and Deb drove five hours each way to visit me at her house, a gesture I still can't think about without tearing up. Dawn, a pastor, has prayed for me when I didn't have the words, then enfolded me in life-affirming hugs. We've also had hilarity, like when Andrew finished his PhD and the rest of us donned choir robes to knight him in a surprise ceremony with a plastic toy lightsaber and the silliest Viking helmet ever made.

Every summer when we meet, our gatherings are marked by great conversations about books, as we watch the kids play on the beach or we all drive to area attractions. And every summer, we clamor for Andrew to make his famous jungle chicken, based on changing

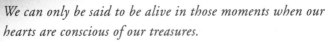

We can only be said to be alive in those moments when our hearts are conscious of our treasures.
—THORNTON WILDER

ingredients on hand. Whatever he puts in it, it's always delicious.

Gratitude practically tackles me when I'm on vacation with these people. This year, toward the end of a particularly busy summer, our reunion gives me a week simply to stand back and appreciate God— and these friends who have taught me so much about God. One day, a group of us heads out to pick Michigan blueberries. It's a perfect day, the sun high against a powder-blue sky, the fields stretching forth in promise. We pop the berries, sun-kissed, plump, and sweet, into our mouths and our buckets, chattering all the while. At one point, alone and shielded by the greenery of the high bushes, I raise my arms in gratitude for this most perfect day, for these friends, for the simple joy of fruit and harvest. Blueberry buckle tonight, blueberry pie tomorrow. Thank you, God.

benedictine hospitality

All guests who present themselves are to be welcomed as Christ,
for he himself will say: "I was a stranger and you welcomed me."
— ST. BENEDICT

I had an experience of real hospitality some years ago when I was visiting the Badlands for a week with family and friends. My mother's favorite cousin lives in South Dakota, where he is a brother at a Benedictine abbey. Mom had given me his contact information long before I left on the trip, but between the day trips and vacation plans we'd made with friends (what is an abbey compared to Mount Rushmore and the Wall Drug store?), I'd never called to inform David I was coming.

I phoned him, guiltily, on our final morning. I expected him to tell me he was busy, justly irritated by my breach of etiquette. Instead, the conversation went like this:

"Hello, David? I mean, Father John? This is Jana Riess, um, your cousin Phyllis's daughter."

There was a brief silence, and I realized that David may have been preparing himself for sad news. I had never called him before, and he and my mother are now of an age where unexpected phone calls from the younger generation rarely bring good tidings.

"Mom is just fine," I rushed to add. "I'm actually calling, because, well, I'm visiting friends about an hour away from you, and we'd love to come and see you if you have some time."

"Ah, wonderful!" he cried. "When do you think you'll be coming?"

"Well, actually, I'm afraid it would have to be today. We're flying home tomorrow morning, and I'm sorry I never called before. . . ."

"Ah, wonderful!" he cried. "Will it be you and your husband?"

"Yes, the two of us, plus our daughter that you haven't met yet, plus another couple," I said awkwardly. "There are five of us in all."

"Ah, wonderful!" he cried. "We don't get nearly enough visitors here. Let me give you directions. Can you be here in time for lunch?"

Before I hung up the phone, David had made me feel like he had woken up that morning just hoping against hope that a ragtag band of loosely confederated idiots would descend on his monastery that very day, and he simply couldn't wait to show them around. It was a sensibility that lasted for our entire visit. He gave us a tour, introduced us to fellow monks and parishioners (he is also a parish priest), fed us a handsome feast for lunch, and answered all our questions about monastic life. He bounced my daughter on his knee and chatted with us as though he had all the time in the world.

And the thing is that David is insanely busy; anyone could see that. The challenge of many monasteries today is that monks are older and their numbers fewer, and yet they still have all the duties of running the monastery and the guest house, and making cheese or fudge or wine or whatever it is they produce to sustain themselves. It gets harder every year to make a go of things. Add to that David's responsibilities in the parish, and it becomes clear that he has no lack of things to do and places to be. Yet to him, nothing was as important as making visitors feel as welcome as Christ himself.

If we hadn't got Christ's own words for it, it would seem raving
lunacy to believe that if I offer a bed and food and hospitality to
some man or woman or child, I am replaying the part of Lazarus
or Martha or Mary, and that my guest is Christ.

— DOROTHY DAY

It's humbling to be on the receiving end of that kind of hospitality, and I can only imagine how difficult it must be to engineer it. This month, though, I'm going to try.

THE RULE OF ST. BENEDICT

David's hospitality didn't spring up overnight. As we were leaving the abbey, marveling at the day, one in our group observed that we'd all just experienced Benedictine hospitality in action. "He's been formed by that for decades," my companion said.

"That" turns out to be the Rule of St. Benedict, the basic guideline for any Benedictine monastic community. Written around 540, it's not very long—about nine thousand words—but covers everything from work (everyone has plenty) to sleep (nobody gets enough) to care packages from home (sorry, but you have to share). The Rule can be surprisingly practical and specific; Benedict seems almost as concerned about the state of his monks' footwear as he does about the state of their souls. But you can tell that every guideline arose out of specific problems and situations. It's like with parenting; you don't create the rule about not eating popsicles in the house until someone has dripped sticky orange goo all over the carpet.

I need to remind myself of the Rule's practicality because, like many people, I have a knee-jerk reaction against the word *rule*. I think I have adult-onset Oppositional Defiant Disorder. Actually, scratch the "adult-onset" part. I've always been this way. I don't like other people telling me what to do, how to behave, how to live my life. Who does? In the family I grew up in, people who followed others blindly were regarded as lemmings. "Imbeciles," my father called them. I had to look that word up. The messages of childhood were clear: question authority, be a critical thinker, don't take any wooden nickels. At least in one way I am healthier than my father: he hated institutions and the people in them. I am suspicious of institutions but I love people.

In Benedict's time, a monastery was small enough—a dozen monks or so—that it felt more like a family than an institution. So maybe this "rule" of St. Benedict is like those house rules every family has, some written and others unwritten. Put the toilet seat down. Clean up after yourself. Don't run the lawn mower in the house. (Don't ask, but that is indeed a rule in our home.)

Benedict's Rule is far-ranging, but his most famous statement is probably the one that opens this chapter—that every stranger should be welcomed as Christ. This is the aspect of the Rule I'm zeroing in on this month. Through the centuries, Benedictine monks have lavished hospitality on wayfarers. When the theologian Dietrich Bonhoeffer visited London in the 1930s, he was blown away by the reception he got when staying at a local monastery. "The natural hospitality, which is evidently something specifically Benedictine, the really Christian respect for strangers for Christ's sake, almost makes one ashamed," he wrote to his best friend, Eberhard Bethge. "You should come here some time! It's a real experience."

This month, I'm not joining a monastery, but I'm going to look out for opportunities to practice hospitality. I want to be more like my mother's cousin David and less like—well, less like me. In one month I can hardly expect to be as formed by the Rule of St. Benedict as David has been, but surely I can venture out of my comfort zone to understudy the role of Christ for a few wayfarers.

HOSPITALITY DONE RIGHT

As September begins, I immediately find hospitality being practiced in an unexpected place. One day I undergo my not-quite-annual gyn exam and find, to my amusement, that the doctor has placed two homemade cozies on the stirrups that hold my feet.

"Did you make those yourself?" I joke with her.

"Actually, yes, I did," she says sheepishly. I am touched by this. Like eleven out of ten other women, getting a gyn exam ranks right up there with a root canal on my list of Happy Things to Do Today, but here is my doctor trying to make my feet warm and comfortable by knitting stirrup cozies. She probably doesn't even know she's practicing Benedictine hospitality, but she clearly wants to welcome the stranger as Christ, should our Lord ever need to visit the doctor.

My friends Ray and Roberta have also taught me about hospitality. They were strangers to me until the 1990s, when I was researching what would become my dissertation. I needed to take a research trip to a far-off city and asked my friend Angela, who came from there, if she knew of a dormitory or cheap motel close to the archives.

"Don't stay in a dorm," she said. "You can stay with my parents."

"Oh, no," I protested. "I've never even met your parents, and this is going to be a ten-day trip, maybe even two weeks. Nobody wants to have guests for that long. Guests and fish start to stink after three days. Remember?"

Angela is stubborn as well as fiercely kind. She insisted that her parents would be thrilled and made all of the arrangements. True to her word, Ray and Roberta were delighted to open their home to me, and we became fast friends. Now I stay at their house whenever I'm in town, which is often, and I always know that I'll be loved in every detail: that the red fleece robe and hunter green slippers will be hanging in "my" closet, that we'll enjoy memorable conversations and delicious meals, that I'll be enthusiastically licked by their Bernese

Mountain Dog, the third in a series of Berners they've had since I first met them. Walking over the threshold of their peaceful house feels like I've come home.

And isn't that what we all want, what hospitality is about? It's being welcomed at the table, with others who are genuinely glad we're there. The grandeur of the welcome isn't important; making the effort is. When I was a graduate student, I was always impressed by the meals my friends could conjure out of their Lilliputian Manhattan apartments. One couple had a studio that probably wasn't even three hundred square feet total, but they were constantly inviting folks over for dinner and to spend the night. They called it their "Stay-Free Mini-Pad" and made jokes about its tiny size even while squeezing eight in for dinner and rolling out the futon for friends of friends looking for a place to crash in the city. I always enjoyed spending time with them.

NOTE TO SELF: DON'T BE LIKE SODOM

Sometimes we can't quite put our finger on what it is that makes us feel welcome, but we're usually keenly aware of such details in reverse—when we perceive a *lack* of hospitality, we can identify exactly what went wrong. Once, I arrived in a college town to speak at a summer conference. I was on the last train, and although I had e-mailed my arrival time to the conference organizers in advance, no one came to pick me up, and the organizers weren't answering the cell phone number I'd been given. After almost two hours, someone finally fetched me from the station, but by this time the cafeteria had closed for the day and no one had thought to save any food for me. The organizers seemed too harried to care. I ordered a pizza, but waited nearly an hour for delivery because the organizers hadn't told me the name of the dorm where I was staying and, weirdly, that information wasn't posted anywhere. I had no map of the campus and didn't know how to give the pizza guy directions, but he finally found the dorm after seeing me standing outside waving my arms like a banshee. Famished, I devoured half a lukewarm pizza and climbed into a hard dorm bed that had sheets but no blanket.

Things only got worse the next day, when the conference program demanded participation in spiritual rituals that made some people uncomfortable, including me. It involved lots of chanting and moving around in circles to release "negative energy."

Of course, my whole perspective of the conference was colored by the fact that no one had met me at the train station and I went to sleep shivering. How might my experience have been different if someone had met basic needs and shown an interest in getting to know me? Hospitality is about more than seeing to visitors' nourishment and comfort, although that's a hugely important start. It's about welcoming the stranger so that the stranger is no longer strange. He or she becomes known as a person. When that happens, lives can be changed, friendships formed—even wars averted.

In the Old Testament, laws of hospitality demanded that guests be given protection, an important consideration in a violent tribal culture where people might just as soon hack you into pieces as open the tent flap to let you in. It's funny how our modern interpretations of the Bible have downplayed the critical importance of hospitality in some of those stories, especially in the book of Genesis. We think it's sweet that Abraham entertains angels-in-disguise in Genesis 18, and we give him kudos for killing the fatted calf and all that. But we don't usually connect that story to the chapter that follows, in which those same angels go to Sodom and almost get drawn and quartered by an angry mob. Lot is spared from the city's fiery destruction because he's the only guy in all of Sodom who gives shelter to these angels (who are still traveling incognito) rather than trying to harm them.

In our time, we tend to interpret the text as focusing on the "sin of Sodom"—a sexual thing. Our forebears even invented the word *sodomy* to describe this sin, in hushed tones of course. But in the Old Testament, extending into the time of Jesus, these chapters were read in a totally different way. They were about a community's failure to show hospitality to strangers, and the serious divine wrath that resulted from this neglect.

Sodom and its neighboring town Gomorrah were destroyed not because men were having sex with cows or with each other—despite the unfortunate fact that the word *Gomorrah* sounds like a venereal disease—but because their people tried to kill God's messengers. In the Gospels, Jesus refers to Sodom and Gomorrah when he's teaching the twelve disciples how to go out into other towns to preach the gospel and heal the sick. If anyone won't welcome them, he says they should "shake off the dust" from their feet and leave that place, because it will be "more tolerable for the land of Sodom and Gomorrah on the day of judgment than for that town" (Matt. 10:14–15).

Clearly, God cares about hospitality. A lot. Since I'm not hankering to be burned to a crisp like Sodom, I ought to pay attention and practice being more hospitable, more Benedictine. But how?

WOULD I FRIEND JESUS ON FACEBOOK?

"Jane Doe wants to friend you on Facebook," the message announces. All I have to do is click on the link, and presto! Jane and I will suddenly become BFFs. In the past, I have been careful to say no to every one of these requests from people I didn't know personally or couldn't identify in a police lineup should that need ever arise. If I had time, I would add a prissy little note: "I am so sorry to have to refuse your kind offer of Facebook friendship. I have a rule that I only friend people I have personally met. Perhaps one day I'll be lucky enough to meet you in person, and then we can be Facebook friends as well as face-to-face friends." Subtext: *I don't kiss on the first date, people.*

Now, however, I am going to friend promiscuously. If St. Benedict were online, he'd hardly demand the *bona fides* of every wayfarer who attempted to scale his Facebook wall, would he? So I start small, by accepting invitations from two people with whom I have friends in common. Really, how different is this than being introduced to them at a party? After a few days of this, the sky has not fallen in, so I accept a few more invitations. Soon I am racking up the Facebook friends.

On the one hand, this is a good way to force me to literally welcome the stranger. A colleague of mine has pointed out to me that the default mode of Facebook is friendship. You are given the opportunity to confirm a relationship (or ignore a request), but by using the language of confirmation, Facebook already assumes that a relationship exists. Somehow I think Benedict would approve of this.

The problem with the Facebook experiment, though, is that I'm still in total control of these "relationships." I can friend people but then hide them in my news feed so I don't have to hear about the ten pounds they've just lost (only fifteen more to go! they squeal), or the way their toddler threw up on them last night, or how many new crops they've just planted in some inane-sounding application called Farmville.

The truth is that I don't want to know these things. I don't want to invest in the lives of perfect strangers—who, incidentally, are called "perfect" strangers precisely because it's only when we investigate others up close that we're privy to their many flaws. I can barely assimilate the flood of Facebook information I am already getting from people I care about. Those are people to whom I have an abiding attachment, either because we are friends in adulthood or because, as is the case with one of my Facebook friends, we once had to pee together in a dirt hole in Guatemala when there was no toilet to be found. You can't help but bond after an experience like that.

I'm aware that the roots for *hospital* and *hospitality* are the same; both come from the Latin root *hospes*, for foreigner. We get a number of other English words from that same root—*host, hostel, hospice*, even *hotel*—but all of them share the core idea of welcoming the stranger into our physical midst. What all this dictionary hunting tells me is that my Facebook experiment is fine insofar as it goes, but I'm not exactly risking anything here. It's time to open our home to guests.

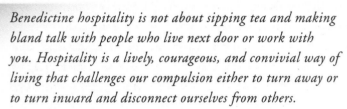

Benedictine hospitality is not about sipping tea and making bland talk with people who live next door or work with you. Hospitality is a lively, courageous, and convivial way of living that challenges our compulsion either to turn away or to turn inward and disconnect ourselves from others.
—FATHER DANIEL HOLMAN AND LONNI COLLINS PRATT

WELCOMING THE STRANGER AND THE FRIEND

"Would you mind taking Patches for a few days?" inquires my friend Shay, a confirmed dog lover like myself. She and her family are heading out for a long weekend, and they can't bring their pound dog of dubious ancestry (part miniature Doberman/part beagle/100 percent insane) with them. Aha! A genuine hospitality opportunity. I readily agree.

When Shay drops Patches off, she confesses that the dog recently got into her son's medication and has been having a touch of diarrhea. "But I don't think it will be a problem," she reassures me as she heads out the door. And I believe her, because Shay is a doctor, and doctors wouldn't minimize symptoms like diarrhea. Would they?

They would.

Patches turns out to be a pooping machine.

She poops outside when and where she is supposed to, yes. But for good measure she also poops on the kitchen floor, in the basement, in my office, and on the carpeted landing. She poops in out-of-the-way places, like under my desk, probably because in normal times she *is* a well-trained dog who knows that it is forbidden to conduct such business in the house. Phil and I resort to confining her to the kitchen when we're asleep or out of the house, but she doesn't take to that one bit, whining and scratching for release. She craves our company and does not wish to be alone.

So it probably shouldn't surprise us when one day Patches makes a run for it. We've become spoiled with Onyx, who is the laziest dog in Ohio if not the entire United States of America. Onyx could be off leash his whole life and never give you a moment's anxiety. We've forgotten what real dogs can be like. They actually run after squirrels instead of sniffing in their wake with serene interest.

Patches senses her freedom when Phil is hooking up Onyx at the front door for the dogs' walk, and she's out like a shot, leash trailing and bumping behind her. What ensues is a madcap Tom-and-Jerry chase scene in which Phil, Jerusha, and a neighbor give hot pursuit. "Catch her!" Phil cries to the neighbor, who hastily jumps from his porch and attempts to grab the leash. But Patches is too fast for them, streaking ahead with exuberant zeal. It takes four people a full twenty minutes to get the dog to succumb to a bribe of grilled chicken.

I've missed the whole fiasco because I'm on a business trip. I'm sorry that I left my family to bear the brunt of my hospitality experiment, but also secretly relieved to have missed the hunt, as well as some of the pooping and subsequent cleanup.

"You owe me big-time," Phil declares grimly upon my return. It's not just the dogsitting he's talking about; my family is also about to visit, along with our friend Edward from England. Phil loves them all, but for an introvert all these visitors are just overwhelming. He needs some space.

It's the first time we've ever hosted Edward, though he's been to visit my mom and we've all been to England to visit him. If you were to try to choose the world's most easygoing person on whom to practice your hospitality, Edward would fit the bill. Though nearing seventy, his activity level puts me to shame (A ten-mile hike with other pensioners? No problem!). Still, he's old enough that nothing quite fazes him. There's an air of bemused tranquility about him.

The visit doesn't quite begin according to plan because I've managed to forget that Edward is a vegetarian. How did I overlook that? I once gave him a copy of *The Moosewood Cookbook*, for heaven's sake, and yet I've cooked a chicken for his first night and planned a roast for tomorrow. So thoughtless. Instead, Edward eats a can of split pea soup for his first meal with us, but at least I can rescue dessert: I've made a delicious sour cream pound cake, the fussy kind where you have to separate the egg yolks and then whip up the whites until they're stiff but not dry. For once, I did it just right. The cake is perfection.

"Oh, thanks so much, but none for me," Edward declares after his tinned soup. "I don't really eat sugar, much."

Not . . . eat . . . sugar? *This* is news.

"Oh!" I reply, startled. "Is this a new health restriction?" How awful for him.

"Well, no, I just never developed a taste for it."

"Really, nothing? No cake, no cookies, no candy . . . ?" It is a sign of how saturated American culture is with sugar that I am desperately sympathetic for his plight. I try to remember back to our visit to England. Come to think of it, Phil and I were the ones downing Cadbury chocolate after almost every meal. I don't recall Edward joining in.

Phil attempts a stab of humor, carrying forward a running joke about Edward's age. "What, they didn't have sugar way back when you were a kid?" he laughs. Edward does not laugh.

"Actually, that's right. There was no sugar to be had in the shops until I was about ten, and by then it just tasted terribly sweet to me and I couldn't get on with it at all," he explains. World War II for him meant, among other things, a childhood with no sugar. Jerusha thinks it sounds like something out of a grisly fairy tale.

Throughout Edward's long visit, he continues to politely decline the sweets, perhaps with a twinkle in his blue eyes. For me this engenders a valuable lesson in hospitality: making guests feel welcome is about allowing them to be who they are, not who you want them to be. I want Edward to join me in having a brownie, or perhaps eleven, but this is not his identity.

I understand that one dimension of hospitality is not trying to change people, but sometimes that's not easy. After Edward has been with us for several days, my mother and brother join us. Mom and Edward resume a friendship that has spanned four decades, since she was an exchange student in England in the 1960s. It's a rare treat to spend time with my big brother, who's perfectly lousy about keeping in touch though he will occasionally deign to text me. Yet I've forgotten how much his smoking bothers me; I hate the smell that lingers by the back door, on his clothes, in the trash can where he's dumped his butts. John knows that he can't smoke in the house, and he's always respectful of that rule. He's also aware that I don't approve of his smoking, if my hundreds of subtle hints through the last twenty years are any indication.

"You know those things are going to give you lung cancer," I chide him during his first evening. He has lugged his latest ginormous history book out to the deck and is settling in for a smoke and a nice long read. His brown hair, released from its ponytail, tumbles forward into his eyes. He probably wants to be alone to read and enjoy the sunset, but he is too sweet a person to say so.

"Nah. That's why I smoke this healthier brand, Natural American Spirit," he responds. This repartee is our comforting, ongoing ritual. "No additives. Those additives can kill you, man."

This is the part where I'm supposed to make a witty comeback about how I've heard about a minor ingredient called nicotine that can exterminate you, too. Instead, I provide him with an ashtray to use on the deck, and bring forward the most comfortable chair. It's a small gesture, but I can tell he appreciates it. He knows I haven't suddenly embraced the fallacy that smoking is great for him, but I want him to feel comfortable in my home, to feel loved. And to come back.

My small efforts at making my friends and family feel comfortable in our home are pleasant, but I have a nagging suspicion that they are superficial. What becomes increasingly clear as the visit progresses is how appallingly busy Phil and I are. Real hospitality requires a certain flexibility, and flexibility requires time. I, on the other hand, have an ironclad to-do list at the start of each day, and I keep having to cut short a conversation or beg off a sightseeing visit in order to produce, accomplish, cross things off. (Apparently I retained little spiritual value from my month of Sabbath keeping, because although I don't work on Sundays, I still define myself by the old Pharaoh standard of productivity.)

I sense that Edward thinks that Americans are ridiculously over-scheduled, and he's right. I had hoped to take more time off for his and my family's visit, but by the time the date long circled on the calendar actually arrives, I'm behind in my work and have to forego a couple of day trips just to catch up. We do try to do things together in the evenings, like going to Eden Park to see a free outdoor production of *As You Like It*. During the daytime, though, my family's life feels relentlessly overprogrammed.

My master is of churlish disposition
And little recks to find the way to heaven
By doing deeds of hospitality.
—WILLIAM SHAKESPEARE, *As You Like It*

Edward is very understanding, but I know I'm not living up to the Rule of St. Benedict, which wants me to receive every guest as I would welcome Christ himself. The truth is that if Christ *did* knock on my front door seeking entrance, I'd have to pencil him in for sometime in the future, like maybe when I am retired or dead.

I'm enjoying Benedictine hospitality more than almost any other practice I've attempted this year, but I also mourn the loss of private time. Instead of vegging out in front of the TV in the evening or retreating to my room with a book, I feel I should engage our guests in conversation or plan something for their entertainment. The strange thing is that while I suspect at least some of them would prefer to be left alone and I'd rather have some time alone too, I can't quite give them that space. What am I, a control freak?

I've been on retreats at Benedictine monasteries before, and part of the joy is in how much they leave you to your own devices. If you want to talk with a monk or spiritual director you can, but you have to request it. If you want to meet other retreatants, you can eat dinner in a room designated for conversation; if not, you can read a book or sit in silence during dinner and no one thinks it's rude. I love the freedom and flexibility of the monastery, but it's harder than it looks to create that do-as-you-please environment for my own guests. They have such different needs. My mom would like nothing better than to talk all evening; my brother wants to play a computer game; Edward would probably like to read but seems open to other activities, so is easy prey when Jerusha comes hunting for someone to play cards with her; Phil wants to work on the bathroom renovation; and I would enjoy curling up to watch *The Daily Show* before bed.

Around the time I'm feeling spiritually deficient for not being the perfect embodiment of Benedictine hospitality, I receive an encouraging message from an old seminary friend I haven't heard from in years. In reconnecting, she does more than remind me of old times; she helps me return to the core of what hospitality should be about. She and her husband, now Methodist pastors, used to be frequent guests at our apartment for dinner, especially our annual "widows and orphans" Thanksgiving potluck, which she remembers fondly.

"Your houseful of people who had nowhere else to go for the holiday has actually shown up in our sermons several times as an example of the Kingdom of God!" she writes. "But, if imitation is the highest form of flattery, then I guess I'll tell you this . . . because of you and Phil, each year we make it a point to invite people to our dinner who will be alone on Thanksgiving. We have a tiny place (as you remember) but so did you when you hosted it. This year, we will have 13! We will be borrowing tables and chairs from church and having a great day. Thank you so much for the influence you both had on our life and celebration."

Hospitality is a gift that keeps on giving, as other people pay it forward in a spirit of cascading generosity. My hospitality doesn't have to be perfect to be effective at helping people feel loved. It is through hospitality that we come to know one another and maybe even glimpse the face of God. I'm reminded of the fact that after his resurrection, Jesus' own disciples didn't recognize him until after they had broken bread with him. It was only following a shared meal that they truly saw him.

I think St. Benedict is on to something.

what would Jesus eat?

It behooves us, therefore, piously to venerate the piety of that blessed man [St. Francis], by whose marvelous sweetness and power ferocious beasts were quelled, wild animals tamed, and the nature of brutes, rebellious to man since his fall, was sweetly inclined to his obedience.

— ST. BONAVENTURE

"Let me get this straight." Lauren peers at me through her Far Side glasses, her eyes intense as she regards me with equal parts exasperation and amusement. "You're going to stop eating meat altogether?"

"Well, just for one month. And then I think I'm going to go back to eating meat, but on a much smaller scale, with several vegetarian meals a week," I say.

"You already don't drink alcohol and coffee, and you don't smoke," Lauren points out. "Now this. Are you *ever* going to get to do anything fun?"

I'd like to reply that I'm a barrel of laughs despite my abstemious lifestyle, but it occurs to me that if you have to point out to your close friends how fun you ostensibly are, you're probably not all that much fun. But Lauren loves me, quirks and all. She listens as I explain why I'm going to spend a month avoiding my good friend, Mr. Porterhouse.

It all started a couple of years ago when I went to a luncheon sponsored by the National Humane Society. Over the meal, our crowd of journalists watched a brief documentary about factory farming while we ate a lunch that looked and tasted suspiciously like it had been concocted from the very chickens we saw being oppressed on a large screen. I actually stopped eating the main course, and when the announcement was made during dessert that the meal had actually been a grain-based chicken substitute, I was relieved to have spared Clucky even while I regretted not getting to finish my portion before it was cleared away.

The documentary was eye-opening. One scene showed a suckling pig being torn from its mother, both of them literally screaming at the forced parting. I wanted to flee the room. The film also showed some of the pens that pigs are kept in. The pigs had no room to move from side to side, nowhere to lie down, no way to scratch themselves—only six inches of extra space in which to step forward or backward in their cages during their entire adult lives—lives that clearly weren't destined to end well.

Although the documentary was undoubtedly propagandistic, it made an impression. I'm a small-town Midwesterner by rights. I grew up not far from Kewanee, Illinois, the proud Hog Capital of the World, where every Labor Day weekend the residents grill and serve fifty thousand pork chops. All around western Illinois, pig farms with hundreds of tiny lean-tos rested in the fertile black earth. Every hog was the king of its domain, with a hut of its own and plenty of room to wander the farm. I had naively imagined such blissful independence to be normative for pigs.

You have just dined, and however scrupulously the slaughterhouse is concealed in the graceful distance of miles, there is complicity.

—RALPH WALDO EMERSON

So, for the month of October, I'm not going to eat any meat, though as an entrenched milkoholic I reserve the right to binge on milk, cheese, yogurt, and eggs. I expiate a portion of the guilt by buying cage-free eggs, but there's no way I'm ready for Vegan Prime Time. Eliminating meat from my diet is enough of a sea change for the moment.

ST. FRANCIS

Although what pushes me into vegetarianism is an inflamed social conscience, I'm eager to explore its religious roots. Plenty of people take on vegetarianism because of their political or social beliefs, but what about vegetarianism as a spiritual practice?

October kicks off with a beloved annual tradition—taking Onyx to be blessed. On a sunny Sunday afternoon, we all head over to Phil's church to join a parade of dogs, cats, gerbils, hamsters, and assorted reptiles. The event is always held on the church's front steps so that passersby can grab a quick blessing while Fido's out for a walk. After the congregation sings some kid-friendly ditties about creation, the priests go around the crowd and pronounce lovely blessings on each animal, invoking the saintly benediction of St. Francis, whose feast day this is.

I've always liked St. Francis, the patron saint of animals. My friend Judy has a modest sculpture of him in her garden, flanked by a lamb at his side and a dove on his shoulder. It's reassuring to know our furry friends have their own patron saint. This month, I am going to read St. Bonaventure's classic biography of St. Francis, which is the first saint-on-saint biography I've ever read. It turns out to be hagiography in every sense of the word: naturally, the book wants to portray Francis in the best possible light, as does any hagiography worth its salt. But since it's written by Bonaventure, who was destined to become a saint himself, it proves incapable of criticism. It's a positively treacly biography. I guess such generosity of character explains why Bonaventure got to be a saint, and why I never will.

I get a fuller picture of Francis's early life, which includes the more controversial pieces, by reading other biographies. Apparently shortly after his death in 1226, unauthorized works began appearing that were a little too forthcoming about Francis's youthful, preconversion debauchery. Bonaventure's 1260 biography represents the church's official attempts to put the kibosh on these more colorful accounts of wine, women, and song.

The basic contours of Francis's life story remind me of the Buddha's: both men were born into moderately wealthy families, learned the centrality of pleasure, and became what we might call partiers in young adulthood. However, both came to recognize the aching emptiness of even the best things this world has to offer. Once awakened to the suffering of others, both made a spectacular show of rejecting wealth and the fathers who had taught them to love it, the Buddha by fleeing his father's palace for a life of asceticism and Francis by stripping naked in the town square and returning his fancy clothes to his angry, astonished father.

Although I'm curious about voluntary poverty, for my purposes this month, it's Francis's unique relationship to animals that interests me most. Francis's life was filled with animal-related stories, which are ideal subjects for the many children's books that have been written about him. (The story about him stripping naked is entirely absent from these picture books, incidentally.) In one tale, Francis saves a village that's been terrorized by a killer wolf. The villagers have almost bankrupted themselves by sending a knight and then an army to kill the wolf, but to no avail. Francis is able to disarm the predator, *Super-nanny* style, just by gently explaining to "Brother Wolf" that it's not polite to devour children. He succeeds because he's able to communicate with the wolf "in its own language" (Wolfese? Romulan?) and see things from Brother Wolf's point of view. The villagers agree to set out plates of food for the wolf, and Francis goes on his merry way, having resolved the crisis and saved the town.

In another story, Francis was traveling with a group of monks when he spied a flock of birds resting nearby. Francis decided that he needed to preach to the birds, because really, who was speaking the good news to winged creatures in the thirteenth century? His fellow monks reported that the birds were attracted by Francis's words, "and suddenly all those also on the trees came round him, and all listened while St. Francis preached to them, and did not fly away until he had given them his blessing." Francis preached to them about how God had clothed them with his care, preserved their species in the ark, and given them nests. He warned them against the sin of ingratitude, which was apparently a particular temptation for birds. But the birds loved the homily:

> As he said these words, all the birds began to open their beaks, to stretch their necks, to spread their wings and reverently to bow their heads to the ground, endeavouring by their motions and by their songs to manifest their joy to St. Francis. And the saint rejoiced with them. He wondered to see such a multitude of birds, and was charmed with their beautiful variety, with their attention and familiarity, for all which he devoutly gave thanks to the Creator.

After Francis had blessed the birds and made the sign of the cross in the air, the birds all arranged themselves into four companies according to the four directions of the cross, and flew off to carry this good news to the ends of the earth.

It's a lovely story, and there are many others like it. But the most surprising element my research turns up is this: Francis might have then baked those sweet gospel birds into a pie. For even though Francis is listed at famousveggie.com as one of history's most famous vegetarians, even though I have already devoted my month of Christian vegetarianism to his saintly memory, he was an omnivore. In one place, for example, he lauded the joy of Christmas by saying that on that holy day, Franciscan friars should receive a double portion of meat in celebration. This apparently happened even if Christmas fell on a Friday, which was traditionally a meat-free day. (Never one to forget the animals, he also advocated livestock receiving a double portion of hay, at least until such time as they became Christmas dinner.)

St. Francis was not actually a vegetarian. Oh.

I admit I am surprised. Consider this quotation from St. Francis I find at the Christian Vegetarian Association website: "If you have men who will exclude any of God's creatures from the shelter of compassion and pity, you will have men who deal likewise with their fellow men." It hardly sounds like Francis would be ordering the rib eye at the Outback Steakhouse. I guess I had just assumed.

Part of the problem is that the whole concept of full vegetarianism is anachronistic. In the first-century church, Christians abstained from meat on Wednesdays and Fridays, but not all the time. As I learned in my month of fasting back in February, many Eastern Orthodox churches still fast on Wednesdays and Fridays, though in the Catholic West it became primarily Fridays and some special holy days.

Even Jesus chowed down on Brother Fish from time to time. Come to think of it, Jesus conjured several *thousand* fish to feed the hungry multitudes. If he had cared deeply about vegetarianism, he could have fed the five thousand with just some loaves of bread and miraculously reproducing pomegranates, and then offered a clever parable about not skewering and roasting our animal friends. But he did not.

I know it shouldn't bother me to learn that St. Francis, like Jesus, was likely not a vegetarian. The very word *vegetarian* didn't enter anyone's vocabulary until the nineteenth century, and as scholar Stephen Webb has pointed out, what passed for historical vegetarianism was as often rooted in a hatred of the body's natural functions as it was in a desire to treat animals with more respect. I imagine that being mendicants played a part; since Francis and Jesus depended on the hospitality of others and beggars can't be choosers, they would have eaten whatever was put in front of them. Just the idea that Francis regarded animals as brothers and sisters was a radical departure from the norm in his day—and our own.

Still, my inner child feels betrayed. I actually stop reading about St. Francis's life—a shallow response, but an honest one. I am disappointed in him. I recall my friend Judy's sculpture of St. Francis standing next to a lamb. Was he imagining how Sister Lamb might taste with mint sauce?

For Francis, the emphasis on animals was about more than eliciting a warm-fuzzy feeling about warm, fuzzy creatures. To him, animals symbolized Christ's incarnation—God's willingness to enter into the dung heap of this world just to be one with us. It's no accident that Francis is credited with starting the first live nativity scene way back in the thirteenth century. He wanted people to experience the whole Christmas story with a cast of real livestock, in all their braying and crapping complexity. That, to him, was the world of Jesus who was Immanuel, not a demure wooden crèche scene.

I suspect in my heart that vegetarianism points to this enmeshed, meddling Jesus who wants to live among us and sacralize everything. To this Jesus, even the birds of the air and lilies of the field warrant honor in God's kingdom. Francis was on to something when he regarded the animals (and the moon, and the sun, and everything else in creation) as brothers and sisters. This Jesus did not weigh animals by their usefulness to human beings, or count them as mere instruments in a strict hierarchy of creation. This Jesus did not apparently question, as many of my fellow humans have done, whether animals have souls. He welcomed them as an integral part of the kingdom of God.

THE LUKEWARM VEGETARIAN

If both Jesus and Francis believed that animals had souls, who am I to serve my furry friends for supper? When I'm honest with myself, which happens once or twice a year, I admit to a deep unease about my carnivorous ways. Eating animals feels immoral to me, and I've been ignoring the promptings for too many years. I need to give up meat.

But just because I'm on board with the idea of vegetarianism as a spiritual practice doesn't mean I'm practicing it perfectly. Vegetarianism, it turns out, is more difficult than it looks. I've made salads, soups with vegetarian stock, and enough pasta to feed Francis's home nation of Italy. I've also indulged in my favorite lunch of a grilled cheese sandwich and cream of tomato soup at least twice a week. I never thought I would tire of it, but I can't quite face bright red liquid again. I have also consulted the nutrition label for the first time and realized that the soup has enough sodium to kill a small animal, or possibly me if I try to sustain a vegetarian lifestyle from a can. So I eat more salads than usual, which makes me feel healthier but still hungry.

After two weeks of semi-virtuous eating I am seriously craving a burger. I won't let myself have one, but I do bypass the Fresh Market in favor of the Golden Corral, a chain buffet restaurant that Phil and I have nicknamed the Golden Trough. Since he and I both hail from lower-middle-class backgrounds, a part of us will forever pine for the stick-to-your-ribs comfort food that comes from places like The Trough. Down-home people want their vegetables clothed in butter as the good Lord intended, not sitting there perfectly naked for all to see.

I don't want any more waif food, no greens or granola. I miss the four-way at Skyline Chili. I want fried chicken, and if I can't have that, I'm going to have the Trough's macaroni and cheese along with green beans that were probably boiled with a nice chunk of ham for flavor. The specter of ham technically violates this month's principles, but since it is only a suspicion, maybe I'm not morally responsible for the welfare of Wilbur, or whichever pig might be gracing my vegetables today.

I can think of several compelling, logical reasons not to eat animals, so it's odd that I can't stop remembering how delicious they are. First, it's bad for the environment, because it takes so much grain to feed the kinds of animals I love to eat. To raise the grain, we have to cut down trees, contributing to greenhouse gasses and a loss of biodiversity. I've read one statistic that says eating a pound of meat is the same as driving forty miles in a gas-guzzling SUV. Second, it's not great for my health. Meat today comes with a host of nasty chemicals and growth hormones, not to mention old-fashioned health risks like clogged arteries and high cholesterol. (Granted, the idea that vegetarianism is healthier is based on an optimal veggie diet of salads and nuts, rather than the actual diet of fettuccine alfredo I've resorted to, but for the sake of argument let's just assume I am the very model of a modern vegetarian.) And of course, the third reason is the not terribly kind treatment of the animal in question. At the end of the day, I feel less of a person, and less a follower of Jesus, when I stab a steak knife into a juicy slab of medium-rare prime rib. That was somebody's son.

THE COURT OF PUBLIC OPINION

I can't seem to completely follow through with my own ideals—my culinary memories are inextricably tied up with meat as comfort food: chicken noodle soup, pot roast with gravy, turkey at Thanksgiving. With the ideals of St. Francis (even if not, apparently, his deeds), I'm committed to defending vegetarianism in principle. What's more, I have naively assumed that most people share my sense that we all *should* be vegetarians. It turns out I'm largely mistaken about this. When I talk to people about my month of vegetarianism, some are supportive, even impressed, like when I tried to fast. Still, a surprising number disapprove.

Several male acquaintances, as well as my husband, ask whether I'm getting enough protein. Why are men so obsessed with protein? It's as though my vegetarianism had personally threatened their muscle buildup. This, however, is tame compared to the response of one outspoken elderly woman in my church, who shakes her head in outrage when I mention my vegetarian experiment.

"The Scriptures are clear that we're supposed to be in charge of the animals," she quarrels. "I just don't know *what* the world is coming to. Besides, what will happen to all those animals if we don't eat them?"

I'd like to report that I hold my tongue out of Christian patience, but my silence is more the result of being too shocked to speak. This woman often has that effect on people. It's her ministry.

How can I explain to her that "those animals" would never be bred in the first place if demand for their meat declined? That the image she has in her mind—the same image I used to share—of happy cows roaming the fields doesn't take into account the fact that nearly half the meat in the United States was raised on factory farms?

I stop asking other people their opinion of vegetarianism.

Maybe I should follow Francis's example and talk to the animals, asking them what they think. I start with Onyx, because he's the member of the animal kingdom I know best, and we already understand each other's language.

One evening I test Onyx's principles by offering him a hunk of the chicken breasts I've poached for Phil's and Jerusha's enchiladas. Tonight's enchiladas are carefully divided into two Pyrex dishes, a large one with a yellowish *M* on top in melted cheese, and a petite dish for me with a *V*—for vacillating vegetarian.

"Here you go, buddy," I tell Onyx, dangling a morsel of chicken as he sits patiently before me. Ever polite, he does not lunge or jump up like other dogs. But his decorous manners don't extend to refusing the chicken, even if it belongs to a fellow animal. He seems pretty copacetic with the whole thing, actually, downing it quickly and looking up hopefully for seconds.

This is not the response he offers when I replace the chicken with the vegetarian strips I'm putting in my own enchiladas. He chokes one down, then lumbers away to occupy his usual command post at the foot of the stairs. Not a success.

AMISH CHICKEN

Vegetarianism in theory is something I wholeheartedly support; vegetarianism in practice is tough to implement. It's another failed spiritual practice, since I can't even quite make it to the end of October. Eating in an upscale restaurant the last week of the month, my eye lingers on the "Amish chicken" on the menu.

"What makes a chicken Amish?" I ask the waiter.

He looks flustered. He is not aware that the chicken has any unique religious sensibilities.

"That just means that the chicken was raised by the Amish, with no growth hormones, in a humane environment," he explains, gazing a little too long at his order pad.

"So it's a free-range chicken?" I persist.

"Yes, I think so. Free-range. From an Amish farm." He does not meet my eye.

"Do you know how it was slaughtered? I don't mean to put you on the spot, but that kind of thing is becoming pretty important to me." My friend and dinner companion, Anna, is now rolling her eyes at my interrogation.

"No, I have no idea how it was slaughtered, but I can tell you that the chef prepares the breast of the chicken in an orange tarragon sauce. It's a specialty dish," he concludes, as if that settles the matter.

It does. I'm that cheap and disgraceful. I am lured, just like that, from all my vegetarian ideals by the promise of a chicken that was raised in a "humane" manner more befitting the eighteenth century than my own. I've since learned that almost everything the waiter told me about Amish chicken was likely a fabrication; many Amish use growth hormones and chemicals, and some raise their poultry in solitary confinement coops for the bulk of the birds' lives. But ignorance is bliss, and by the time my succulent meal arrives I have already named my chicken Brother Yoder and imagined for him an enviable prerestaurant life. Before I eat him, I picture Brother Yoder ranging around his farm in a black hat and suspenders. All the other chickens show up with tiny hammers on a Saturday to help him build his coop. He has a beautiful, peaceful life until one day—only when he is very, very old—he knocks on the kitchen door of the Amish homestead and indicates that he's ready to make the leap from farm to table.

The fantasy, and the bird, go down well. Someday I hope I will have the courage of conviction I need to resist the siren smell of bacon and give up meat altogether. St. Francis can pray for me. In the meantime, I'm definitely going to cut back. Starting mañana, or maybe the next day.

~~seven~~ ~~five~~ three times a day will I praise you

Prayer is as variform as any other human activity. The Liturgy of the Hours, or the Divine Offices, is but one of those forms, yet it is the only one consistently referred to as "the work of God." The Divine Hours are prayers of praise offered as a sacrifice of thanksgiving and faith to God and as a sweet-smelling incense of the human soul before the throne of God. To offer them is to serve before that throne as part of the priesthood of all believers. It is to assume the "office" attendant upon the Divine.

—PHYLLIS TICKLE

I used to work from home for a magazine that required me to travel frequently to conferences and trade shows, where I would see my colleagues and enjoy their company. One of my coworkers, Phyllis Tickle, would frequently disappear at lunchtime for a few moments, something I never wondered anything about until one day she explained to us what these mysterious absences involved.

"I'm praying the hours," she said simply.

Not coming from a liturgical background, I needed a remedial explanation of what this meant. What secret ritual required her to disappear to a hotel or convention center bathroom at noon each day? What were "the hours"?

My curiosity was piqued, mostly because I adored Phyllis. If she had been snorting cocaine in the bathroom, I'd have wanted to try it too. Mostly I wondered if fixed-hour prayer had helped Phyllis to become the person she is—a living saint, but with a rare sense of humor. *If so,* I thought, *sign me up for that.*

This was a decade ago, and Phyllis has done much to revive and popularize the ancient spiritual practice of praying the hours. Her multivolume series *The Divine Hours* came out while we were still working together, and it was a joy to hear her speak about the practice and to meet others who had taken it up. But I've never tried it myself in any sustained way. Now, armed with the autumn-season edition of *The Divine Hours* and some supplementary books to help me understand the practice, I'm ready to start another adventure.

RETRO PRAYER

The practice of praying at fixed times during the day has a number of different names—the Divine Office, the Divine Hours, the Liturgy of the Hours. I'm just calling it fixed-hour prayer because "office" sounds bureaucratic. Although Phyllis mentions becoming an "attendant" for God, this feels a bit secretarial, and God can fetch his own cup of coffee.

I'm part of a pretty low-church Christian tradition, where people are encouraged to pray every day but there's no fixed formula for doing so. We don't recite the Lord's Prayer in our church services, and as far as I know most people don't do this regularly in family prayer either, though I haven't exactly conducted polls. I expect that many people in my church are suspicious of "rote" prayers, which smack of Catholicism and might lead to Pharisaic vain repetition. We're certain that vain repetition will cause dogs and cats to start mating with each other, and that will bring about the end of the world.

However, fixed-hour prayer is not something that the Christian church invented after Jesus; it comes from Judaism. "Seven times a day I praise you," says Psalm 119. There's considerable evidence that Jews prayed at fixed times throughout the day, and the practice became so widespread that by the age of Jesus and the Apostles it was firmly entrenched. By then, Jews were living in the Roman Empire, and their prayer routine accommodated the empire's rhythms. In the Roman understanding, a day was cut into two parts—6 AM to 6 PM, and 6 PM to 6 AM. So prayers are set for the third hour (9 AM, or "terce"); the sixth hour (noon, or "sext"); the ninth hour (3 PM, or "none"); and so on.

According to Phyllis, the New Testament gives some interesting hints about how fixed-hour prayer was practiced in Jesus' time. "The first detailed miracle of the apostolic Church, the healing of the lame man on the Temple steps by Sts. Peter and John (Acts 3:1), occurred when and where it did because two devout Jews (who did not yet know they were Christians as such) were on their way to ninth-hour (three o'clock) prayers," she writes. "Not many years later, one of the great defining events of Christianity—St. Peter's vision of the descending sheet filled with both clean and unclean animals—was to occur at noon on a rooftop because he had gone there to observe the sixth-hour prayers."

This new information fascinates me. Though I'm familiar with this story from the book of Acts, I'd been so bowled over by its fantastic vision of pigs hurling themselves at Peter that I'd ignored this particular detail. It strikes me that Phyllis is right: Peter was on the rooftop to pray. The book of Acts goes out of its way to tell us what time it was. "In Joppa and far from Jerusalem and the Temple, Peter had sought out the solitude of his host's rooftop as a substitute site for keeping the appointed time of prayer," she explains.

Jesus practiced fixed-hour prayer too. New Testament scholar Scot McKnight says that Jesus was an observant Jew, and "it was customary for pious Jews to interrupt the day to pray at three separate times"—generally morning, afternoon, and evening (Ps. 55). This was in addition to all those times that Jesus went off by himself to pray privately; his prayer life combined both spontaneous personal prayer and fixed-hour prayer based in the Psalms. A balanced diet.

No way am I going to be able to do this seven times a day, though. The math of that is downright chilling. Prayer seven times a day gives you forty-nine weekly prayer opportunities: at 3 AM, 6 AM, 9 AM, noon, 3 PM, 6 PM, and 9 PM. You'd get to sleep from about 9:15 PM until 2:45 AM. Five and a half hours of sleep a night. No wonder so many monks took vows of silence; they would have been biting each other's heads off out of grumpiness otherwise. Instead of praying through the night, I plan to quit with compline, the last prayer ritual of the day, at 9 PM. Compline says good-bye to the cares of the day and prepares us for rest; it is as quiet and pure as a lullaby.

I am going to do five of the daily offices, and I task my trusty iPhone to remind me. I set it for 9 AM, noon, 3 PM, 6 PM, and 9 PM, using the "Chimes" ring that comes standard on the phone. Somehow its carillon-inspired music seems appropriately monastic, even if the sound is a bit tinny.

FLEX·HOUR PRAYER

I'm drafting an e-mail and the phone goes off. I'm in the middle of making dinner and the phone goes off. I'm driving Jerusha to flute lessons and the phone goes off.

Now the duty of having stated times of private prayer is one of those observances concerning which we are apt to entertain . . . unbelieving thoughts. . . . It is easy to see why it is irksome; because it presses upon us and is inconvenient. It is a duty which claims our attention continually, and its irksomeness leads our hearts to rebel.

—CARDINAL NEWMAN

Somehow I had imagined that I would be better organized at this. I'm a planner by nature, a list-maker who gladly sits down each morning to plot out the day. So why am I consistently taken by surprise when three hours have passed and it's time, *already*, to delve into fixed-hour prayer?

I know that there's no rule that says I can't start praying at 12:04 or 9:07, but on the other hand there's a certain grace in dropping whatever I'm doing and forcing myself to pray exactly on schedule. I'm supposed to be molded and shaped by this practice, not reinvent it to suit my own needs. Prayer should order my daily life, not be ordered around *by* it. Part of the problem I've had with a regular prayer routine in my years as a Christian is that I try to squash it in each day between all of those other "important" things on my list, and of course half the time it doesn't happen at all. This month, prayer is supposed to be the main course, not the optional dessert.

I start out faithfully, obeying my cell phone chime by pulling out *The Divine Hours*, which has a lovely satin ribbon to mark my place from three hours before. For days I trip happily from terce to sext to none to vespers to compline, missing a service only rarely. The language is gorgeous, I realize. Why have I not tried fixed-hour prayer before?

Each office includes the same basic elements—a call to prayer, a request for God's presence, some short Psalm passages, the Lord's Prayer, and sometimes a hymn or short reading from the Bible. It doesn't take much time to read each short service aloud: five minutes if I'm moving hastily or fifteen if I take the time to try to sing the Psalm portion. I've never officially learned how to chant like this, but

If you sing to God, you pray twice.
—ST. AUGUSTINE

since no one but God will hear me singing, I figure it doesn't matter that I don't understand the visual cues the text offers for making my pitch go up or down. I muddle through. Mostly, I'm proud of adhering to Benedict's Rule that instructs people to "immediately set aside what we have in hand and go with utmost speed" to pray when the signal comes. I am actually succeeding at a spiritual practice!

Then I travel to Montreal for a conference. I've packed not only my large autumn and winter edition of *The Divine Hours* but also a handy pocket version that tucks easily into my laptop bag. (Why isn't there a smart phone app for fixed-hour prayer, I wonder?) I feel ready to take this spiritual practice on the road. Yet somehow the quiet contentment of praying the hours at home vanishes into the ether in the face of back-to-back meetings from breakfast until late at night.

Part of the pleasure of being on the road is seeing friends I don't often get to spend time with. Do I want to pray the hours at 6 PM, or head out to dinner with Kelly and Donna? No contest. I float off to dinner without praying the vespers service first. When I return to the hotel room that night, I fall into bed exhausted, too tired to pray the compline service or even look at a prayer book.

This mode of prayer is rapidly becoming inconvenient.

There are all kinds of interruptions and excuses. I have to travel today and will be on an airplane; chanting there may well be interpreted as an act of terrorism. However, that St. Benedict is a crafty old coot. He clearly foresaw my "but I'm traveling" excuse and inserted the following in his Rule: "Those who have been sent on a journey are not to omit the prescribed hours but to observe them as best they can, not neglecting their measure of service." There goes that loophole. I could mouth the words in-flight, but decide instead to skip it, just this once.

However, "just this once" bleeds readily from one day to the next. I excuse myself entirely on a day I'm going to be in meetings from 9 AM to 5 PM, and driving two hours each way before and after. And several times, I'm in situations where my cell phone is turned off, so I miss the prayers because I don't hear the chime alarm and forget about my allotted prayer time. After my trip to Montreal I figure I'm batting about .400 with fixed-hour prayer.

My initial enthusiasm fading and the guilt piling up, I decide to adhere to Phil's family motto ("If at first you don't succeed . . . lower, lower your standards!") and revise my ambitious schedule to just three times a day. It's what Jesus and the apostles probably did, after all, and I wouldn't want to be setting myself up as holier than they were. That would be prideful, and pride is bad.

What's more, I will give myself the flexibility to decide which three of the hours I'll be doing on any given day. I basically forget the noon service altogether, because I'm always in the middle of something and wind up feeling resentful—not the most spiritual attitude for prayer.

THE CRY OF THE CHURCH

Once I've dialed down my expectations, I settle into a less erratic rhythm for fixed-hour prayer. Or rather, it begins to settle its rhythm on me.

I'm surprised by how comforting I find its repetition. I've never recited the Lord's Prayer this often in my life, but far from being empty words, the prayer exerts an unexpected power. Praying for daily bread *every day* is quite different from praying for it almost never (as in my church) or once a week (as in my husband's). It communicates trust in God for today. Just today, we have a blue-light special on manna; only one per customer, though, so you'll need to ask again tomorrow if you want more.

There's also a reassuring cadence in the antiquity of these prayers. That's not to say I agree with everything I'm praying. Some of the assertions made in these Psalms are hard for me to swallow at face value—when the psalmist says that the Lord "guards the lives of his faithful; he rescues them from the hand of the wicked" (Ps. 97), for example, my eyebrow is raised. God does not *always* preserve the lives of his saints. He does not *always* deliver them from evil. Yet praying the Psalm out loud in the knowledge of all the millions who have prayed it before, regardless of their fates, has unexpectedly tempered my innate skepticism. We voice what we *hope* will be true, and we pray that God will save us, delivering us from evil. The prayer is not hollow, because it has voiced both the agony and the trust of countless generations.

The purpose of prayer is not to get good at it, but for the Church to become good through it.
—SCOT MCKNIGHT

Fixed-hour prayer is an exercise in inhabiting the communion of saints, that great cloud of witnesses of all those, living and dead, who pray with us and for us. I feel connected, plugged in, to something larger than myself. This comes home to me most clearly in the middle of the night. Despite my resolution not to wake up at 3 AM like a religious fanatic to pray the lauds service, I find myself doing so—not because I have suddenly become a superhero of righteousness but because the insomnia that plagues me episodically hits for about ten days near the end of November. My bouts with insomnia tend to last a week or two, then recede for a few months, and then return without much rhyme or reason. I will usually go downstairs to watch TV and have a snack—two of the activities, incidentally, that sleep experts tell insomniacs never to do. I don't usually mind the insomnia keenly because I enjoy the solitude and the way the house is so quiet. I'm the only one awake besides Onyx, who follows me anywhere no matter what time it is.

Phyllis has a special book called *The Night Office* that becomes my friend during this time. I am still doing my usual nocturnal activities when I can't sleep, but now I'm also reciting the Office of the Night Watch (3 AM matins) or the Office of Dawn (6 AM lauds), depending on what time I am awake. The repetition is as soothing as warm milk with honey. "I commune with my heart in the night," says Psalm 77, which is used as a frequent refrain in *The Night Office*. The mood is contemplative, brooding. "Darkness is not dark to you; the night is as bright as the day," says another refrain (Ps. 139). God is with me in the darkness.

In both day and night, fixed-hour prayer helps me to fall in love with the Psalms all over again. I'm reminded of the truth of what everyone always says about the Psalms: that they contain in microcosm the entire range of the human experience. There's pain, jealousy, pettiness, and anger; desolation, abandonment, and despair. But there's also joy and praise and shouting. All of this sometimes happens within the same group of Psalms, or even within the same Psalm—check out Psalm 119 for a neck-whipping example of how God either redeems the whole of the human experience, good and bad, or the psalmist is relentlessly bipolar. Possibly both.

WHEN WE DO NOT HAVE THE WORDS

During my fixed-hour prayer experiment, I come across a wonderful book by Robert Benson called *In Constant Prayer*, in which he describes his discovery of the Divine Office in middle age and the fifteen years he's spent softly planting this particular prayer garden and watching it bear fruit.

Benson opens the book by introducing Bettie, a friend of his who is known as something of a prayer warrior. "Bettie would say something like, 'Jesus, help Alan's back to feel better in the morning,' and in the morning Alan's back would feel better. Or she'd say, 'Jesus, help Robert not to worry,' and the next day I would not be so anxious. One day, after six days of torrential rain, she said, 'Jesus, we need good weather tomorrow for traveling home,' and the rain stopped before any of us had time to say amen. I swear it did, and I have witnesses."

The problem for Benson, and I suspect for me as well, is that his prayers rarely turned out the way Bettie's did. Miracles were not forthcoming; healings failed to materialize. For a time, he blamed this on himself and his lack of faith. After struggling more, he began to blame it on God, who did not appear to listen. "I have come to believe that it was because I was trying to say Bettie's prayers, not the ones I could say," he writes. His own spontaneous prayers often came up empty, like mine. They felt hollow.

What has filled the gap for him is fixed-hour prayer, which is "prayer for the rest of us," prayer for when we do not have the words. As someone heavily invested in language, I find that liberating. Six days a week, I try to come up with words: bits of sections of chapters of books, written piece by piece; new blog posts five days a week; dozens of e-mails a day. Maybe one reason I'm enjoying fixed-hour prayer so much is that it gives me a break from the me-me-me nature of my own spontaneous prayers. There is a deep rest associated with ancient prayers I didn't contrive myself.

But it's even deeper than that, because in fixed-hour prayer I am finding to my astonishment that I am most myself when I pray someone else's words. Given that my faith tradition suggests that following someone else's liturgy can be empty and confining, I'm surprised to discover that instead it is rich and freeing. I don't have to be alone with my subjective experience, my little life. I am free to rest in the words of those who are often far wiser, and who have walked this path already.

SO IT TURNS OUT I'M A SINNER

In my primarily low-church tradition, we don't talk about sin much as an existential category of being; sin is something we step into sometimes, but it doesn't necessarily define who we are. We believe we fall short and need to repent, but we don't dwell heavily on the idea that we are born sinners. That's even more true in American culture, where the only time we're likely to hear the word *sin* is in a sentence about a particularly rich chocolate cake.

With fixed-hour prayer, the liturgy pays far more attention to sin than I am used to. It's inherent in the Lord's Prayer when we pray not to be led into temptation. It's implied in last week's "cry of the church," which is "Lord, have mercy on us. Christ, have mercy on us. Lord, have mercy on us." In this week's cry, we're supposed to call out, "Oh Lamb of God, that takes away the sins of the world, have mercy upon me." We wouldn't exactly need all that mercy if we weren't standing ankle-deep in our own excrement.

You'd think that this emphasis on sin to a person who isn't used to hearing it would make me feel even worse about myself than I already do for failing at all these different spiritual practices this year: like a child with doting parents who's always been told he was a good kid suddenly being spirited away to a rotten boarding school where he's beaten with a switch and forced to eat tripe with a spork. In truth, however, the emphasis on sin comes as a relief, like having a boil lanced. It's painful, but you know it's necessary or your knee will just keep swelling to an ungodly size and the infection will spread throughout your whole body. I already *know* I am a crappy old sinner, even while everybody keeps telling me, in and out of church, that I'm a basically nice person. They're wrong. If I learned anything this year, especially from the Jesus Prayer back in June, it's that I'm a selfish worm.

It's decent of the liturgists to tell me the truth about myself.

It also helps that they're not abandoning me to wallow in sinnerhood, like I felt after reading Jonathan Edwards's "Sinners in the Hands of an Angry God" in the eleventh grade. I didn't take literally Edwards's metaphor of the spider hanging just above the licking flames of hell, but the image made a profound impression. What was the point in trying *not* to be a sinner, if you had little or nothing to say about your own salvation anyway because God had already played eeny-meeny-miny-moe with your soul and you lost?

Fixed-hour prayer emphasizes sin, and the liturgy doesn't shy away from discussing hell; it's in the Psalms and the Gospels, after all. But it leaves me with a completely different feeling, like I've taken a scalding bath and emerged, red-skinned, to find that God has warmed a towel especially for me.

The cold stones of the Abbey church ring with a chant that glows with living flame, with clean, profound desire. It is an austere warmth, the warmth of Gregorian chant. It is deep beyond ordinary emotion, and that is one reason why you never get tired of it.

—THOMAS MERTON

By the time Thanksgiving comes, I am fully a convert to fixed-hour prayer. So far this year, the specific practices I've discovered that I most want to continue are the Jesus Prayer and this one. Both have called out to some deficit deep within my soul, a scarcity I sometimes felt in a hopeless way but could not, or did not dare to, articulate.

My stats for fixed-hour prayer are still dismal, so by ESPN standards, the month is another failure. In the thirty days of November, with seven prayer opportunities per day, I could have prayed the office 210 times. I've probably completed only a fifth of that. But numbers don't tell the whole story: I feel closer to God and to the communion of saints. That's got to count for something, because it feels like it means everything.

generosity

[Jesus] said that a glass of water given to a beggar was given to Him. He made heaven hinge on the way we act toward Him in His disguise of commonplace, frail, ordinary humanity.

—DOROTHY DAY

"Um, Mrs. Smith? May I please speak to Mrs. Smith?"

That's when I know I am screwed. The only people who call me Mrs. Smith are strangers who don't realize that my husband and I, in a fit of impractical postcollegiate egalitarianism, both kept our original last names when we got married. This starched voice belongs to a telemarketer, and the telemarketer must belong to a charity, because all noncharitable telemarketers are blocked from dialing our telephone number. Normally, I would simply thank him for calling, announce in a crisp tone that our family does not accept telephone solicitation, and hang up the phone before he can chime in about saving puppies or the planet. But today I cannot. This is the first day of December, so I must hear his spiel to the bitter end. Then I'll be obliged to give him something.

It's my month of radical generosity, of giving liberally to all who ask. This comes from the Gospel of Luke, one of those inconvenient passages I try not to think about:

And unto him that smiteth thee on the one cheek offer also the other; and him that taketh away thy cloak forbid not to take thy coat also. Give to every man that asketh of thee; and of him that taketh away thy goods ask them not again. (Luke 6:29–30 KJV)

For December I am putting this verse into action by becoming a girl who just can't say no. And like the one in the Broadway musical, I can already see that I'm in a terrible fix. I am going to have to say yes to this stranger on the phone. What will it be this time? The firemen's ball?

"Um, ma'am? Is this Mrs. Smith?" the über-polite voice persists.

"Yes," I respond weakly. "This is Mrs. Smith. How can I help you?"

"As you know, Mrs. Smith, so many children today are being diagnosed with rare and terrible cancers. The Leukemia and Lymphoma Society would like to be able to count on your help."

Oh my Lord, I think. *He's going to ask me to run the friggin' marathon.* "Since you've been so generous to us in the past"—which is generous of him to say of my microscopic and erratic donations—"we would like to ask you to be a neighborhood cheerleader for the society. If we send you some fundraising letters and envelopes, could you address them and distribute them to your neighbors?"

That's it? I exhale with wild relief and accept eagerly. "Yes! Yes, absolutely I can do that." There is a brief silence on the other end while he contemplates the sincerity of my 180-degree turnaround from appeal dodger to MVP for the Kids. But I had been sure he was about to ask me to run the marathon, since my earlier donations had come when various well-toned friends had pounded the pavement to fight children's cancers. I was content to support them from the background, writing checks while munching on Oreos. Addressing a few envelopes seems like an awfully small request compared to twenty-six miles of hellish agony.

My goals for this month are two:

1) to give to anyone who asks (and I do mean anyone, so as I continue my haphazard November practice of praying the hours I insert a few ad hoc petitions that I not be solicited by the KKK, Rush Limbaugh, or the John Birch Society, on the far right; or anything to do with Al Franken's new political career, on the left); and

2) to raise $4,000 for charity. This last goal is in conjunction with my fortieth birthday this month. The birthday feels significant; a corner is being turned away from young adulthood and into middle age. I'm far from having a midlife crisis, but I do sense a settling weight of yearning, or wanting my life to have mattered to more people than my immediate circle of family and friends. I also feel, at this threshold of forty, tremendously blessed in said family and friends. I want to give back.

BE THE CHANGE

On December 1 I log on to Facebook to register for a brand new way to pester my friends. Inspired by a blogger I know named Jana (yes, a different Jana), I want to use Facebook Causes to ask my friends for charitable contributions in honor of my birthday. Earlier this year, Jana, who lost one of her legs to cancer as a teenager and now walks with a prosthetic, raised money for state-of-the-art prosthetics for a twelve-year-old girl in China who had lost both of her legs in the Sichuan earthquake. Jana's original goal was $380 in honor of her thirty-eighth birthday. This was increased to $600 and then $1,000 after friends' donations poured in. I think all of us donors felt the power of what Jana was doing; we were raising money for a cause that was important to her, but we were also celebrating her survival.

How wonderful it is that nobody need wait a single moment before starting to improve the world.

—ANNE FRANK

What I didn't realize was that Facebook would make me choose just *one* cause. Do I want to stop violence in Darfur, or cure cancer? Do I want children born with a cleft palate to have access to surgery, or to save the arts in public schools? Faced with so many needs, it's hard to know where our donations might make the most difference.

I finally decide on the Heifer Project International. My conservative friends will poo-poo this as a circuitous way for liberals to imagine they are improving the lives of people they'll never meet. My liberal friends will chafe at the consumerist mentality Heifer has, in which donors "buy" an animal for a community in the developing world (or, if we're really swinging out, a whole flock). And that's not even considering the folks I probably offended in chapter 10 by my inability to become a vegetarian, the ones who will be horrified that Heifer teaches people how to raise animals for meat as well as wool and eggs. ("The Heifer Project literally puts a *price* on animals' heads," sniffs one animal rights website.) In short, the Heifer Project has something to offend everyone even while doing good in the world. That makes it my kind of Flunking Sainthood charity.

It feels strange and a bit uncomfortable to lobby my friends for money. Are they going to resent this? Will my request be artfully ignored? I draft a letter that I send out to all my Facebook friends over the next several days:

Friends,

As many of you know, I am writing a book for which I take on a new wacky spiritual practice each month. Well, it's December, which is the season of giving, right? So in the spirit of the holidays, and in honor of my 40th birthday, I am trying to raise a total of $4,000 for various charities, one of which is Heifer Project International (heifer. org). Heifer has been helping families become self-sustaining for 65 years. For just $10 you can buy a share of a goat to help a hungry family. For $120 you can go hog wild and purchase a whole pig!

Won't you please take a moment to make a small donation in honor of my 40th? I don't want gifts or cards. I want you to buy some chickens, people! (And I promise not to do this every year.)

I set my fundraising goal at $800, seal the deal by buying a pig, and wait for my friends to respond.

My sweet friends outdo one another in zeal, as the Scripture says (Rom. 12:10). By the end of the first day of December I'm already a quarter of the way there, and within a week I've zipped past the $800 goal. All in all, thirty of my friends cough up $1,160 on Facebook. According to the charity's website, that means we have provided the equivalent of a water buffalo, a pig, a sheep, a llama, and a goat; four flocks of chicks, four of geese, and four of ducks; two trios of rabbits; and three hives of honeybees. Heifer also e-mails me on Christmas Day to say that its whole Facebook fundraising effort for December has netted $1,758 so far, which means that my own fundraising accounts for about two-thirds of their Facebook totals. Granted, Facebook obviously represents a minuscule part of Heifer's global fundraising strategy, especially at the holidays, but here's the thing: *I feel fantastic.*

This is the best birthday month ever! Often in the busy weeks of December, I experience a vague unease about the impending holiday season. It's a familiar conundrum: we pledge that Christmas will be less commercial and more spiritual, then watch in dismay as our efforts are obliterated in a single outing to Toys "R" Us. My mid-December birthday is usually spent shopping, baking, and wrapping and shipping packages. This year, though, I put the lists away, build a fire in the fireplace, and roast s'mores with my family. This respite occurs in part because my birthday falls on a Sunday, which I'm still trying to keep as a Sabbath. (Although I doubt that rabbis would approve of the open flame, the fire contributes to the overall sense of shalom.) Larger than the actual day of celebration is the general spirit of unexpected calm that has settled around me. I know this tranquility has to do with the generosity project.

I'm not alone in my charitable deeds, which is a welcome change from most of the other spiritual practices I've attempted this year. In addition to the solidarity on Facebook, the company where I work

Teach us to give and not to count the cost.
—IGNATIUS LOYOLA

part-time has forgone a Secret Santa gift exchange for fellow employees in favor of nonrandom acts of kindness this year. Under the new rules, we receive the name of a person, but it's no longer someone to buy little gifts for (which is a relief because it's always agonizing to find tchotchkes with the right personal touch). Instead we quietly scurry around doing five good deeds in that person's name. People make donations to "Dare to Care" and the "Blessings in a Backpack" program, and send cards and letters to soldiers overseas. One person gets four colleagues to sign their organ donor intentions on the back of their drivers' licenses, and someone else knits scarves for a homeless shelter. At the annual holiday party, amid karaoke and Mexican food, we learn the identities of our Secret Santas. Mine has made a donation in my name to the seminary I attended.

There also seem to be opportunities to give at the check-out line of almost every kind of store. I go to Blockbuster video, and they're collecting for St. Jude's Children's Hospital. Barnes & Noble wants me to buy a book for a child in the Big Brothers/Big Sisters program; I choose *A Wrinkle in Time* by Madeleine L'Engle, one of my all-time favorite reads. When I stop at Petsmart to buy dog food, they want financial help caring for homeless dogs and cats. Plus there are the usual community appeals: the Giving Tree at Jerusha's school, the toy drive at church. I contribute to my friends' Facebook appeals for clean water and a cure for brain cancers.

In the end, though, I don't respond to every appeal like I'm supposed to. It's just too overwhelming: public television, public radio, the food bank, every educational institution we have ever attended. . . . I'm asked to help fight breast cancer and lung cancer and bipolar disorder. Even the Girl Scouts, who have apparently heard how much I like their cookies, make a pitch for their endowment fund. By Christmas week I'm certain that with all of these donations plus our regular tithing I've already met the $4,000 goal, so some of the pleas go unheeded in the rush right before and after the holiday. The one I feel most guilty about is a personal letter from someone I know who has started a foundation for kids in Ecuador and Guatemala. I've been to Guatemala; I can almost see the children's faces. Yet I put the unanswered appeals in a pretty toile box with a lid and try not to think about them.

WHAT IF WE ALL PAID TITHING?

When I was twenty I worked at a Salvation Army camp for a summer. All of us counselors had a great time with the kids, so despite the long hours and a fundamentalist camp director who signed his memos, "Camping for the King!" it was a fun time. (Well, apart from the ulcer and all.)

But I had very little money. At the end of August I came home to Illinois to prepare for my senior year of college. My college was located in a frigid climate, and I no longer had a coat. I'd been meaning to buy one all summer to prepare for my return to Massachusetts, but never got around to it. I hadn't paid tithing all summer, either, but had promised myself a couple of years earlier that I was going to try to take the 10 percent thing more seriously. When I sat down at the dining room table to pay my bills and figure out my financial situation before heading back to school, I had a dilemma: I could pay my tithing, or I could buy a winter coat.

I'd cleared about $1,000 for the whole summer of being a camp counselor, and only had $100 or so of it left after expenses (some of which, admittedly, were hardly necessities—unless it's a necessity to attend the home games of the Milwaukee Brewers on days off). My conscience was tugging at me to act on faith and send that last hundred dollars out to bless the world even though I wouldn't have any money left to buy a coat. I debated about this—what would a measly hundred bucks be able to accomplish? Why wasn't there some kind of student discount on tithing—like that students only had to pay 5 percent instead of 10?

I plunged ahead in faith. I decided to send $50 checks to Compassion International and Bread for the World while putting the coat on a credit card—not the most prudent financial decision, but I was barely out of high school. What did I know?

Maybe more than I do now. When I found a coat, which was warm and lovely and cost $85, my mother unexpectedly swooped in and said she felt she ought to pay for it. Since I'd been paying for my own clothes for years, this generous act was quite remarkable, but I wasn't one to look a gift horse in the mouth. I wore that coat for years, a snug reminder of my act of faith in giving a widow's mite to help the poor.

Do all the good you can, by all the means you can, in all the ways you can, in all the places you can, at all the times you can, to all the people you can, as long as ever you can.
—JOHN WESLEY

That's my one tithing miracle story. I'm sure that many experienced Christians will have a problem with the tidiness of it. I know, I've never liked the mentality of "if you only give, God will make you prosper," or "God will pay you back a hundredfold." I don't think that God works that way . . . except for this one time when he did. Maybe such graces are given to relatively young and inexperienced Christians because they need small miracles in order to continue in faith. Or maybe older, more experienced Christians have become just hardened enough that we no longer recognize the small miracles when they do occur.

I do know one thing: the world would change tremendously if more Christians would tithe. This month I revisit Christian Smith's book *Passing the Plate: Why American Christians Don't Give Away More Money.* Its research is a big fat indictment of Americans who, by just about every standard of measurement, don't give much money to charity. It surprises me because I had always heard that Americans were some of the most generous people in the world. If that's true, then the world is in serious trouble.

The book makes some surprising conclusions about generosity. You'd think that people who earn higher salaries would give a higher percentage of their income than those lower on the totem pole. After all, these folks have a sizeable amount left over after paying for the basics of food, shelter, and clothing, right? Wrong. Those who earn more than $70,000 a year contribute, on average, only 1.2 percent of their income, which is half of the percentage contributed by those who earn under $10,000 a year. Giving goes down even further in those who earn more than $100,000 a year. It's kind of crazy, actually: the wealthier we become, the more we forget the poor.

What's especially depressing about these statistics is that because of something that sociologists call the "social desirability bias"—our innate desire to look better in the eyes of others than we actually are—

many if not most of us actually *over*estimate how much we donate to charity. "It turns out that people have a tendency to say they give more money than it appears they actually do," the authors conclude.

To me, the most exciting part of Christian Smith's book is the opening chapter, which dares to dream about what could be accomplished if American Christians decided to tithe 10 percent of their after-tax income to the charities of their choice. There would be an estimated $46 billion—that's billion with a *B!*—every year for philanthropy. The authors parse that out into dream piles: $4.6 billion could clothe, house, and feed every single refugee in Africa, Asia, and the Middle East; $350 million could provide scholarships for seminarians in the developing world. American Christians' tithing could provide free eye exams and glasses to every child in poverty! We could make sure every person on the planet has access to clean water! I know the authors are just playing Fantasy Philanthropy here, but it's exciting to start the book with a vision of the way things *could* be if Christians were more kingdom oriented, rather than the shabby state of things as they are.

ST. DOROTHY

Dorothy Day was that kind of visionary. I first encountered her writings in graduate school, when I read *The Long Loneliness* for a course on American women's autobiography. In it she tells of her bohemian life during World War I and the early 1920s, of the men she lived with and the child she had out of wedlock—as well as the child she aborted. (That latter fact is why she'll probably never become an official Catholic saint, even though she's already one in popular imagination.) A socialist and labor activist, she was an unlikely choice for the twentieth century's greatest American Catholic woman. Her conversion to Catholicism, beautifully described in the memoir, hinged upon a growing love of prayer and a continuing passion for justice, a zeal she carried over from her radical secular days.

Day's decades as a Catholic, from the mid-1920s until her death in 1980, fueled a fiery combination of progressive social causes like antiwar activism and hunger relief with traditional Catholic piety. She and her mentor, Peter Maurin, founded the Catholic Worker movement, which advocated for the poor and founded houses of hospitality in American cities. Not surprisingly, the movement's growth exploded during the Great Depression in the 1930s. Day lived in voluntary poverty so she could pour all of her energy back into the movement. "Voluntary poverty means a good deal of discomfort in these houses of ours," she wrote. "Many of the houses throughout the country are without central heating and have to be warmed by stoves in winter. There are backyard toilets for some even now [in 1951]."

Reading Dorothy Day during my $4,000 charity experiment is like fetching ice cubes from the freezer just before being told you're actually

It is easy to love the people far away. It is not always easy to love those close to us. It is easier to give a cup of rice to relieve hunger than to relieve the loneliness and pain of someone unloved in our own home. Bring love into your home for this is where our love for each other must start.

—MOTHER TERESA

supposed to generate an entire glacier instead. Suddenly nothing I am attempting seems good enough. What is tithing, when Jesus told the rich young man in Luke 18 to sell all that he had and give the money to the poor? What good does it accomplish to raise $4,000 for people I'll never even meet (and if I am honest with myself, don't particularly want to meet)? Just as with the hospitality experiment, I have carefully controlled the parameters of this month's spiritual practice. I want to give to strangers with the click of a mouse, not get involved in their thorny lives. My own life is complicated enough.

Dorothy Day wrote compassionately about people like me, failed and failing saints who, like that rich young man in the Gospel of Luke, could never quite sacrifice our ease and comfort to follow Jesus. "You can strip yourself, you can be stripped, but still you will reach out like an octopus to seek your own comfort, your untroubled time, your ease, your refreshment," she wrote. I am that octopus. One leg writes a check to alleviate other people's poverty while seven others procure my family's food, bedding, vacations, comfortable clothes, entertainment, furnishings, and transportation. By the standards of my own culture, none of this is ostentatious. In fact, as I smugly pointed out in chapter 5, compared to some, our family lives fairly simply. But am I prepared to sell our house, donate the proceeds to the poor, and embrace voluntary poverty in order to serve God? No way.

In fact, I haven't even managed to raise my $4,000 after all. When I settle accounts at year's end and add up all of the charitable donations I made with the ones my friends offered for my birthday, the total is $3,651.47. That's close, but I didn't quite meet the goal. I'm like those people I criticized in Christian Smith's book, the ones who succumb to the "social desirability bias" by overestimating their own generosity.

"I'm really sorry, Jesus," I mutter out loud. I'm walking up Vine Street downtown, heading toward the public library a few days after Christmas with my hands thrust deep into my coat pockets.

"Ma'am, can you help me out some here? I'd appreciate some change." The woman is sitting at the edge of the brick wall that encloses the main library's courtyard, a sign in front of her saying, "HOMELESS. CAN YOU HELP?"

"Sure," I say, scrambling in my purse to find a bill. If I'd remembered my resolve to give to everyone who asks *before* leaving the house,

I could have had some cash in my pocket for such a time as this. As it is, we chat while I hunt for my wallet.

"It shooore is cold out here today. So you like the library?" she asks suddenly. I look her in the face for the first time. She has chocolate skin and a brown ski jacket of the same hue, those muted shades providing background for a riotously colored green and red reindeer hat with jingle bells dangling from the ends of each antler.

"Yeah, it's one of my favorite places anywhere," I reply, giving her a grubby five dollar bill. She smiles at this but makes no comment. She wants to talk politics now.

"Do you think Hillary would have made a good president?"

"Um, do you mean Hillary Clinton?" Barack Obama has been in office for nearly a year. I like Hillary as much as the next person— wait, make that far more than the next person, since most people basically hate her—but I think the presidency ship has sailed without her aboard. I say as much.

"You got that right!" She guffaws. "Mmm-*hmmm*. She ain't never gonna be president now. But I think she'd be a good one. She don't take shit from *nobody*. You have a great day now, lady, and God bless you!" Her reindeer antlers jingle gaily as she dismisses me with a jaunty wave.

Dorothy Day wrote a Christmas essay in 1945 when she talked about how Christ sometimes appears to people in the guise of the poor. We don't give charity to them because they remind us of Christ, Day said, "but because they *are* Christ, asking us to find room for Him, exactly as He did at the first Christmas." It occurs to me, retreating down Vine Street, that it would be just like Jesus to camouflage himself especially for me as a swearing reindeer lady with a love for Hillary Clinton. For a flash, a single instant, my charity isn't charity but connection. I've made a connection.

"And a Meeeeeeery Christmas!" she calls behind me.

Epilogue

practice makes imperfect

Progress is not an illusion. It happens, but it is slow and invariably disappointing.
—GEORGE ORWELL

Six weeks after I turned in this book, I received a surprising phone call. The father I had not seen or heard from in twenty-six years was dying in Mobile, Alabama. Could I come there to say good-bye? Oh, and one more little question: did I want the hospital to discontinue life support, since he was unresponsive and could not breathe on his own?

I was stunned. The day took on a surreal feeling as I called my husband, called the nurse, called the social worker, called the airlines. His condition was bad, the hospital told me. The pulmonologist wasn't sure if he would even last the night. He was "actively dying" now, having been in the hospital for thirteen days with a progressively worsening COPD, a form of emphysema brought on by decades of smoking.

Within a few hours I got on a plane, and spent most of the flight thinking about the past.

My father left us on a Friday, though I didn't know that at the time. I didn't realize he was gone until Saturday morning, and even then I had a child's faith that he'd come back. That certainty lasted for three days. Mom, ever a pushover for a mental health day from school, had allowed me to stay home the following Monday to avoid the prying eyes and awkward questions of my peers. She'd stayed home from work to get a handle on things. After running some errands, she returned home to find me making cookies in the kitchen to cheer myself up. Now she sat down at the table with a thud of finality and defeat. She had been to the bank, she told me through her tears. He had taken every cent. He would not be coming home.

As I traveled to Mobile, I replayed these scenes in detail for the first time in years. The shock, the pain of his sudden abandonment, the betrayal of knowing that he'd chosen to humiliate us still further by emptying the future of retirement for my mother and college for us kids, still stung. The selfishness of it. The shame.

"I'm not sure I can do this," I told a friend I had called from the airport. I was crying full tilt now, my life upended a second time by this man. "I thought I had forgiven him and forgotten all this."

"How could you forget it?" she countered. "He hurt you terribly. You were only a kid then, right?"

"I was fourteen then. I think I'm only about fourteen years old *now*," I sobbed.

"If you turned around right now and went home, no one would think less of you. You don't owe him anything. You are a good person even if you can't do this," she said.

"I feel like this is a test," I confided. "Today I find out whether I'm really a grown-up, and a Christian. What if I fail?"

I am not much holier than I was before I began,
but I am still trying nonetheless.
—ROBERT BENSON

And so I prayed that God would give me peace and the wisdom to know what to say when I saw my father. By the time I arrived at the hospital, so late at night that I had to enter through the emergency room, a quiet peace pervaded every decision. Within moments I was at his side, shocked at his wizened appearance despite the nurse's warnings over the telephone that he would look far older than his actual age of seventy-one. Shrunken and gaunt, this 117-pound man with the breathing tube didn't seem like he could be the larger-than-life specter I remembered from my childhood. He looked piteous, and it was not difficult to find sympathy crowding out every other emotion. Only his famous beak-like nose had retained its full glory.

Dad lasted two more days, and passed away with my brother John at his side describing some of the twists and turns his life had taken after Dad left us. As John talked to him, a cardinal fluttered outside the window, catching John's attention. He hadn't realized there would be cardinals in Alabama in October. When he looked back at my father, the labored breathing slowed and stopped. Dad was gone.

Here is what I learned from my father's sudden reappearance and death: all of those unsuccessful practices, those attempts at sainthood that felt like dismal failures at the time, actually took hold somehow. They helped to form me into the kind of person who could go to the bedside of someone who had harmed me and be able to say, "I forgive you, Dad. Go in peace." Although I didn't see it while I was doing the practices themselves or even while I was writing the chapters in this book, the power of spiritual practice is that it forges you stealthily, as you entertain angels unawares.

John, Phil, and I spent three days cleaning out my dad's apartment, a toxic wasteland of papers, unwashed clothes, and vitamins stacked to the ceiling. Picking carefully through his things, we began to piece together the lost years of his life, and it was a sorry picture. The man who had left us with full vigor and a pocketful of cash had squandered his health on the smoking habit that would kill him and wasted his money on gambling and porn. Sadder still, there was no evidence anywhere of a friendship or any kind of personal relationship in the twenty-six years he'd been gone. He had chased the idea of making his body live forever, but hadn't invested his heart in a single person. The two photographs we found in his apartment that had been taken since he left our family in 1984 were both of himself, snapped one night when he had a memorable winning hand at poker. That was all.

The life of the spirit is one lived for others. My dad, on the other hand, lived opposed to this principle: he was a grasper, always reaching beyond his present circumstances to chase a dream of easy wealth (we found every conceivable get-rich-quick scheme in his files) or restored youth. He did not invest in eternity. I'm sure that God has forgiven my dad, and I can write with honesty that I have forgiven him too. But I don't want my world to be like his. One way to live the life of the spirit, and offer it to God and others, is through spiritual practices—my daily commitment to implementing a different kind of life.

All through this project I've been hard on myself because of the practices I couldn't do at all (Centering Prayer), the ones I did successfully but pridefully or for the wrong reasons (fasting), and the ones I didn't quite see the point of (Brother Lawrence's mindfulness). But in the end, many of this year's practices helped me when I needed it the most: fasting helped to teach me that this body and this life are not all there is, that there is a life of the spirit beyond food and health and the hundreds of bottles of vitamins we cleared out of Dad's apartment. While I already knew this with my head—I've been a Christian for many years, and I know the drill about eternal perspective—still I didn't understand it in the core of my body. Now I do. I didn't fast perfectly, but I also didn't flunk that practice. I came to understand, viscerally, the larger points: God is infinite; this life is a proverbial drop in the bucket; we are but dust. Fasting is a potent bodily reminder of these things.

Sabbath keeping taught me about time out of time. It occurred to me as I dropped everything to be at my father's bedside that when we truly keep the Sabbath, God can mold us into the kind of people who don't make an idol out of work, which is a particular temptation for me and perhaps a lot of other Americans. Sabbath time is like suspended animation, which is also how everything feels when the death of someone we love topples all our plans. Other practices I attempted, especially fixed-hour prayer, have this same undercurrent. *Your schedule is all very well,* these practices say. *But you have to be prepared to drop everything for God, for others, for death.*

After a death, though, we slowly regroup. We spend a few weeks or months in mourning and then gradually move on with our daily lives, never forgetting the person we loved but quite easily forgetting the way death's intrusion reminded us of our own mortality and unimportance. The Sabbath doesn't allow that, however. It's an enforced weekly shutdown of all our pretensions, a glimpse of eternity in the everyday.

I don't have a tidy moral for each of the practices I tried. One of the main lessons I learned this year, in fact, was that I was delusional for imagining I could master any spiritual practice in thirty days. If I had it all to do over again, I would allow for more time. Like, say, a five-year plan. I was also an idiot for trying so much of this by myself rather than in community. Spiritual practices help the individual, sure, but it takes a *shtetl* to raise a *mensch*. There's a particular kind of hubris in the DIY approach I took to all of these spiritual practices, most of which weren't intended to be tried alone.

And if I did it all again, I would try to stop practicing charity from a distance. One of my greatest failures this year was my careful refusal to get involved. In September, my hospitality was practiced primarily on people I already knew; in December, my generosity was expended on people I would never know. Both were easier, far easier, than welcoming the stranger. But it's the act of loving that marks the true saint. And I *was* able to love my dad, there at the end of his life. I sat by his bedside, held his hand, and prayed the Jesus Prayer for both of us. *Lordjesuschristsonofgodhavemercyonmeasinner.*

If we look for Christ only in the saints, we shall miss Him. . . . If we look for Him in ourselves, in what we imagine to be the good in us, we shall begin in presumption and end in despair.
—CARYLL HOUSELANDER

These are small outcomes from practices that were done far from perfectly. In a culture that stresses perfection, I've often heard the maxim that "good is the enemy of perfect"; in other words, when people of faith aim for anything short of godliness we miss the mark. I've learned the reverse is true: perfect is the enemy of good. I may have spent a year flunking sainthood, but along the way I've had unexpected epiphanies and wild glimpses of the holy I would never have experienced without these crazy practices. A failed saint is still a saint. I claim that *S*-word for myself, even with all my letdowns. I turn to Dorothy Day here, who said that we are all called to be saints, "and we might as well get over our bourgeois fear of the name. We might also get used to recognizing the fact that there is some of the saint in all of us. Inasmuch as we are growing, putting off the old [self] and putting on Christ, there is some of the saint, the holy, the divine right there."

Notes

Chapter 1: choosing practices

Another version of Lucy's story says that Roman guards dug out her eyes with a fork. Also unappealing.

Lauren Winner's thoughts on the wording in Exodus are from *Mudhouse Sabbath* (Brewster, MA: Paraclete Press, 2003), ix–x. Abraham Joshua Heschel's quote about the "ecstasy of deeds" is found in *God in Search of Man: A Philosophy of Judaism* (New York: Farrar, Strauss, and Giroux, 1976), 283.

Chapter 2: fasting in the desert

Gregory the Theologian is quoted in *Eternal Wisdom from the Desert: Writings from the Desert Fathers*, ed. Henry L. Carrigan, Jr. (Brewster, MA: Paraclete Press, 2001), 87. That book is also the source of the story about Theodora of the Desert, pages 96–97, and the quote from Father Moses, page 113.

The Brookhaven study about men's and women's different tolerance levels for food deprivation is reported in "Evidence of Gender Differences in the Ability to Inhibit Brain Activation Elicited by Food Stimulation" at http://www.pnas.org/content/106/4/1249.full. You can also read about it in Randolph E. Schmid, "Study: Women Less Able to Suppress Hunger Than Men," *Huffington Post*, January 20, 2009.

For more on the medieval women saints, see Caroline Walker Bynum, *Holy Feast and Holy Fast: The Religious Significance of Food to Medieval Women* (Berkeley: University of California Press, 1987), esp. 25, 41–43, 76, 122, 138. On fasting and the diet culture, see Lynne M. Baab, *Fasting: Spiritual Freedom Beyond Our Appetites* (Downers Grove, IL: InterVarsity Press, 2006), 24–27 and 133–36.

Scot McKnight's thoughts are from *Fasting* (Nashville: Thomas Nelson, 2009), esp. 19, 51, 117. Portions of my discussion of McKnight's *Fasting* book appeared in a review I wrote for Explorefaith.org: http://www.explorefaith.org/resources/books/fasting.php?ht= "One can be damned alone" is quoted in Baab, *Fasting*, 60.

Synclectica's advice about sleeping on the ground is found in *The Sayings of the Desert Fathers*, translated and introduced by Benedicta Ward (Kalamazoo, MI: Cistercian Publications, 1975), 232.

Chapter 3: meeting Jesus in the kitchen...or not

For more on Brother Lawrence, see the introduction to *The Practice of the Presence of God*, trans. Robert J. Edmonson, Christian Classics (Brewster, MA: Paraclete Press, 1985), esp. 31–32, 38–39, 67–69, 100, 109, 112. Hannah Whitall Smith's quote is found in the introduction to this book (p. 21), and Brother Lawrence's correspondence with the Reverend Mother are in the chapter called "Letters" (pp. 79-120).

Yes, I am aware that the *Cadfael* mysteries are set several centuries earlier than Brother Lawrence, and that they take place in England, not France. So please don't send me e-mails correcting me about it.

I'm drawing here from Margaret Kim Peterson, *Keeping House: The Litany of Everyday Life* (San Francisco: Jossey-Bass, 2007), 13, 37–39, 127. Also, if you are interested in someday cleaning an oven, the book I consulted is Cheryl Mendelson's *Home Comforts: The Art & Science of Keeping House* (New York: Scribner, 1999), 119. Mendelson's book is beautifully written and makes for fascinating reading, even if it will make you feel totally guilty about having a less-than-perfect house.

Chapter 4: lectio divination

The epigraph from Eugene Peterson is found in *Eat This Book: A Conversation in the Art of Spiritual Reading* (Grand Rapids, MI: Eerdmans, 2006), 66. Peterson's story of his dog with the bone opens the book and is found on pages 1-2. The quote about "a way of reading that guards against depersonalizing the text into an affair of questions and answers, definitions and dogmas" is on page 90.

The quote from St. Caesarius of Arles is found in Michael Casey, *Sacred Reading: The Ancient Art of Lectio Divina* (Liguori, MO: Liguori/Triumph, 1996), 28–29. Debbie Blue's is in *From Stone to Living Word: Letting the Bible Live Again* (Grand Rapids, MI: Brazos, 2008), 35.

The T. S. Eliot quote about prayer being "to concentrate, to forget self, to attain union with God" is found in Philip and Carol Zaleski's book *Prayer: A History* (New York: Houghton Mifflin, 2005), 288.

Michael Casey's quote about being "brought face to face with the superficiality of our existing commitment" is in *Sacred Reading*, 97. "Lifelong exposure" is found on page 80.

Chapter 5: nixing shoppertainment

The chapter epigraph is from Richard Foster, *The Freedom of Simplicity: Finding Harmony in a Complex World,* rev. ed. (San Francisco: HarperOne, 1981, 2005), 104. Other Foster quotes are found on pages 109 and 215.

The thoughts on "coveting" in the Hebrew Bible come from Richard Elliott Friedman, *Commentary on the Torah: With a New English Translation and the Hebrew Text* (San Francisco: HarperOne, 2003), 618. This observation also pops up in Abraham Joshua Heschel's book *The Sabbath,* which even gives such repetition for emphasis a fancy name: *epizeuxis.* So now we know. Heschel, *The Sabbath* (New York: Farrar, Straus and Giroux, 1951), 90.

Sheena Iyengar's research is reviewed in "To Choose Or Not to Choose," *The Chronicle Review* in *The Chronicle of Higher of Education,* March 19, 2010, B7–B9, and in her book *The Art of Choosing* (New York: Twelve/Hachette, 2010). The experiments on religion are described in detail on pages 28–30.

Chapter 6: ~~Centering Prayer. er, the Jesus Prayer.~~ look, a squirrel!

The chapter epigraph is from St. John Chrysostom as quoted in *The Philokalia,* "Directions to Hesychasts" 21. The edition I used was translated by E. Kadloubovsky and G. E. H. Palmer, *Writings from the Philokalia on Prayer of the Heart* (New York: Faber and Faber, 1979, 1995), 193-4.

The first quote from Thomas Keating about what Centering Prayer is designed to achieve is found in Keating, *Open Mind, Open Heart: The Contemplative Dimension of the Gospel* in *Foundations for Centering Prayer and the Christian Contemplative Life: Thomas Keating's Three Most Popular Books Compiled into One Volume* (New York: Continuum, 2009), 31. See also 55, 142.

Cynthia Bourgeault's quote about how to undertake Centering Prayer can be found in *Centering Prayer and Inner Awakening* (Cambridge, MA: Cowley Publications, 2004), 6.

"Coloring the air to resemble light" is in *The Philokalia,* Callistos's "Texts on Prayer," item 13, 273.

The idea that we "inhale divinity and exhale sin" is from Zaleski, *Prayer,* 143.

An excellent introductory resource to the Jesus Prayer is Frederica Mathewes-Green's *The Jesus Prayer: The Ancient Desert Prayer that Tunes the Heart to God* (Brewster, MA: Paraclete Press, 2009). She points out that these simple sayings we commit to memory have a profound hold on us at unexpected times: "The things we lay down firmly in our memories *matter.* They endure. If you take the words of the Jesus Prayer and 'write them on the tablet of your heart' (Prov. 3:3), on the day when you are far away on the gray sea of Alzheimer's the Prayer will still be there, keeping your hand clasped in the hand of the Lord" (p. 59). I hope she's right, because when I'm in a nursing home and no longer recall the names of my loved ones, I have a sneaking suspicion that the only thing left to me will be all of the commercial television jingles of my childhood. The Jesus Prayer would be a marked improvement over "Big Mac, Filet of Fish, Quarter Pounder, French Fries. . . ."

Chapter 7: unorthodox sabbath

Readers should be aware that the kind of Orthodox Jewish Sabbath I'm attempting here is hardly the norm among American Jewry. According to the 2000 National Jewish Population Survey, of the 46 percent of Jews who belong to a synagogue, only 21 percent are Orthodox. So it's a small minority who feel they have to preshred their toilet paper or refrain from flicking a light switch on the Sabbath. Among the majority (being Reform, at 39 percent, and Conservative, at 33 percent), there's considerable variation on questions of Sabbath observance.

You can learn about Heschel's life in *Abraham Joshua Heschel: Prophetic Witness*, a thorough and fascinating biography by Edward K. Kaplan and Samuel H. Dresner (New Haven: Yale University Press, 1998).

Heschel's own quotations are from his book *The Sabbath* (New York: Farrar, Straus and Giroux), 13, 23.

For a fascinating cultural study of how various communities of Christians have observed the Sabbath through history, check out Craig Harline's book *Sunday: A History of the First Day from Babylonia to the Super Bowl* (New York: Doubleday, 2007).

Marva Dawn's thoughts are in *Keeping the Sabbath Wholly: Ceasing, Resting, Embracing, Feasting* (Grand Rapids, MI: Eerdmans, 1989), 19. The ideas from Walter Brueggemann are paraphrased from a lecture he gave at the Episcopal Church of the Redeemer in Cincinnati, Ohio, on February 24, 2010.

Chapter 8: thanksgiving every day

The study that found that people who recorded their blessings were 25 percent happier than those who recorded daily annoyances is found in Robert A. Emmons and Michael E. McCullough, "Counting Blessings Versus Burdens: An Experimental Investigation of Gratitude and Subjective Well-Being in Daily

Life," *Journal of Personality and Social Psychology* 84, no. 2 (2004): 379–89, esp. 380–81.

"How can any of us ever be grateful enough for our mothers?" In asking this question I am influenced by Robert Thurman's book *Anger: The Seven Deadly Sins* (New York: Oxford University Press, 2004). He devotes a surprising amount of time to the issue of gratitude to the women who bore and raised us.

Research on how quickly we adapt to change is found in Po Bronson and Ashley Merriman, *NurtureShock: New Thinking about Children* (New York: Twelve/ Hachette Book Group, 2009), 228–29. It's worth noting that Bronson and Merriman state that subsequent researchers have questioned these findings. But, whatever. They work for me.

Margaret Visser, *The Gift of Thanks: The Roots and Rituals of Gratitude* (New York: Houghton Mifflin Harcourt, 2009), 16–17, 58, 226–27. Much of the book discusses the rituals of gift giving, which Visser distinguishes from gratitude: "Gratitude is always about intentions, although it is often expressed through concrete things such as gifts" (158).

Interestingly, customers' tips increase when servers write a note of thanks on the bottom of a bill. See B. Rind and P. Bordia, "Effect of Server's 'Thank you' and Personalization on Restaurant Tipping," *Journal of Applied Social Psychology* 25 (1995): 745–51.

Thomas Merton's words are quoted in *Words of Gratitude*, ed. Robert A. Emmons and Joanna Hill (Philadelphia: Templeton Foundation Press, 2001), 14.

Chapter 9: benedictine hospitality

The epigraph from Benedict is found in the Rule of Saint Benedict 53:1. There are many versions of the Rule in print and available online, such as the one at http://www.ccel.org/ccel/benedict/rule2/files/rule2.html#ch50. (In the spirit of Benedictine hospitality, the Rule's entire text is free to the site's visitors. Welcome!)

Dorothy Day's quotation is from "Room for Christ," December 1945, in Robert Ellsberg's collection *Dorothy Day: Selected Writings* (Maryknoll, NY: Orbis Books, 1992), 95.

The quote that Benedictine hospitality is "not about sipping tea" is from Father Daniel Holman and Lonni Collins Pratt, *Radical Hospitality: Benedict's Way of Love* (Brewster, MA: Paraclete Press, 2002), 9.

The Bonhoeffer quote about staying in a Benedictine monastery in London is from a letter to his best friend, Eberhard Bethge, November 23, 1940.

There are many other references to Sodom throughout the Bible, one of the most explicit being found in Ezekiel 16:49–50: Sodom's guilt was enjoying "pride, excess of food, and prosperous ease" without sharing with "the poor and needy. They were haughty, and did abominable things before me; therefore, I removed them when I saw it." There is some discussion of the Sodom and Gomorrah story in Peterson, *Keeping House*, 13.

Chapter 10: what would Jesus eat?

For accounts of St. Francis's animal miracles and other stories, see Bonaventure's *The Life of St. Francis* in the HarperCollins Spiritual Classics series (San Francisco: HarperOne, 2005).

Stephen Webb's *Good Eating* is an excellent book on Christian ethics and animal rights (Grand Rapids, MI: Brazos Press, 2001). It profoundly influenced my thinking on Christian vegetarianism, convincing me that it's an important and biblical idea, even if it's one I have a hard time putting into practice. See especially pages 128–32.

The quote from Isaac Bashevis Singer is from the short story "The Letter Writer," which originally appeared in *The New Yorker* on January 13, 1968, but is also anthologized in *The Collected Stories of Isaac Bashevis Singer* (New York: Farrar, Straus, and Giroux, 1982).

Chapter 11: ~~seven five~~ three times a day will I praise you

An excellent introduction to fixed-hour prayer is Phyllis Tickle's *The Divine Hours* series, arranged by season. The one I used primarily was *Prayers for Autumn and Wintertime* (New York: Doubleday, 2006). The chapter epigraph is taken from page x, while the story of Peter's noontime vision is on page viii. Fellow insomniacs should check out *The Night Offices: Prayers for the Hours from Sunset to Sunrise* (New York: Oxford University Press, 2006).

The quote on "having stated times of private prayer" is from Cardinal Newman, quoted in Casey, *Sacred Reading*, 22.

The quote from Scot McKnight is from *Praying with the Church: Following Jesus Daily, Hourly, Today* (Brewster, MA: Paraclete Press, 2006), 83.

In chapter 43 of the Rule, Benedict encouraged monks to "immediately set aside" what they were doing and "go with the utmost speed" when the time came for prayer. In chapter 50, Benedict closed a potential travel loophole by insisting that journeying monks were still to observe their regular prayer times. See http://www.ccel.org/ccel/benedict/rule2/files/rule2.html#ch50.

"Bettie would say something like, 'Jesus, help Alan's back to feel better in the morning,'" is from Robert Benson, *In Constant Prayer* (Nashville: Thomas Nelson, 2008), 5–6. The quote about the world not being our personal oyster is on page 58.

Readers who are particularly interested in singing, rather than just reciting, the Psalms will want to look at *Chanting the Psalms* by Cynthia Bourgeault (Boston: New Seeds, 2006), or *The Song of Prayer: A Practical Guide to Learning Gregorian Chant* from the Community of Jesus (Brewster, MA: Paraclete Press, 2009). Both books come with a CD to help readers better understand and listen to the chanting.

Chapter 12: generosity

The chapter epigraph comes from Dorothy Day's essay "Room for Christ," reprinted in Advent devotional I have come to love: *Watch for the Light: Readings for Advent and Christmas* (Maryknoll, NY: Orbis, 2001), 185. The quotation about giving charity not because the poor remind us of Christ but because they *are* Christ is from the same essay, page 186.

Research on American Christians' generosity—or lack thereof—is taken from Christian Smith, Michael O. Emerson, and Patricia Snell, *Passing the Plate: Why American Christians Don't Give Away More Money* (New York: Oxford University Press, 2008), 44, 12–16.

Dorothy Day's quote on voluntary poverty comes from her autobiography, *The Long Loneliness* (New York: Harper & Row, 1952), 187. Day's quote "you can reach out like an octopus to seek your own comfort" is from her 1953 essay "Little by Little," in *Dorothy Day: Selected Writings*, ed. Robert Ellsberg (Maryknoll, NY: Orbis Books, 1992), 110.

Epilogue: practice makes imperfect

Dorothy Day's quotation is from the 1949 essay "Here and Now," from *The Third Hour*, in Ellsberg, *Dorothy Day*, 102-3.

A note to readers

The events described in this book actually happened to me, but I have taken some liberties with chronology to place events in their relevant chapters. As well, I have changed the names of some individuals in the book to protect their identity or, in three cases, created a composite character based on more than one person in order to guard an individual's privacy.

About Paraclete Press

Who We Are

Paraclete Press is a publisher of books, recordings, and DVDs on Christian spirituality. Our publishing represents a full expression of Christian belief and practice—from Catholic to Evangelical, from Protestant to Orthodox.

We are the publishing arm of the Community of Jesus, an ecumenical monastic community in the Benedictine tradition. As such, we are uniquely positioned in the marketplace without connection to a large corporation and with informal relationships to many branches and denominations of faith.

What We Are Doing

Books

Paraclete publishes books that show the richness and depth of what it means to be Christian. Although Benedictine spirituality is at the heart of all that we do, we publish books that reflect the Christian experience across many cultures, time periods, and houses of worship. We publish books that nourish the vibrant life of the church and its people—books about spiritual practice, formation, history, ideas, and customs.

We have several different series, including the best-selling Living Library, Paraclete Essentials, and Paraclete Giants series of classic texts in contemporary English; A Voice from the Monastery—men and women monastics writing about living a spiritual life today; award-winning literary faith fiction and poetry; and the Active Prayer Series that brings creativity and liveliness to any life of prayer.

Recordings

From Gregorian chant to contemporary American choral works, our music recordings celebrate sacred choral music through the centuries. Paraclete distributes the recordings of the internationally acclaimed choir Gloriæ Dei Cantores, praised for their "rapt and fathomless spiritual intensity" by *American Record Guide*, and the Gloriæ Dei Cantores Schola, which specializes in the study and performance of Gregorian chant. Paraclete is also the exclusive North American distributor of the recordings of the Monastic Choir of St. Peter's Abbey in Solesmes, France, long considered to be a leading authority on Gregorian chant.

DVDs

Our DVDs offer spiritual help, healing, and biblical guidance for life issues: grief and loss, marriage, forgiveness, anger management, facing death, and spiritual formation.

Learn more about us at our Web site: www.paracletepress.com,
or call us toll-free at 1-800-451-5006.

Creating with God
The Holy Confusing Blessedness of Pregnancy

Sarah Jobe

ISBN: 978-1-55725-922-6
$16.99, Paperback

The first book about pregnancy written by a clergyperson who's been there.

Creating with God is a boldly truthful, sometimes funny, and deeply spiritual account of where babies come from and where babies take us. Jobe reads the Bible through the lens of her back-to-back pregnancies and invites you to see the image of Jesus in pregnant women, feel God abiding in the work of pregnancy, and to consider the ways that pregnancy can train us in the very practices we need to live a life of faith.

Shirt of Flame
A Year with St. Thérèse of Lisieux

Heather King

ISBN: 978-1-55725-808-3
$16.99, French Flap

If you have not read Heather King before, her honesty may shock you. In this remarkable memoir, you will see how a convert with a checkered past spends a year reflecting upon St. Thérèse of Lisieux and discovers the radical faith, true love, and abundant life of a cloistered nineteenth-century French nun.